PERSON TO PERSON

Derek Bowskill is a freelance writer with a background in theatre, education and broadcasting. He is the author of numerous plays for adults and children and can claim experience in group direction for sensitivity training. He lives on the south coast of England where his hobbies include encountering nature on his boat.

The author is at present doing the research for his new book for Star Books entitled *Swingers and Swappers*.

PERSON TO PERSON

Derek Bowskill

A STAR BOOK

published by

W. H. ALLEN

A Star Book
Published in 1974
by W. H. Allen & Co. Ltd.
A division of Howard & Wyndham Ltd.
44 Hill Street, London W1X 8LB

First published in Great Britain by
Allen & Unwin Ltd. 1973

Printed in Great Britain by
Richard Clay (The Chaucer Press), Ltd., Bungay, Suffolk

ISBN 0 352 01071 1

PREFACE

The research for this book precipitated revealing and illuminating experiences which frequently made me aware of my more than ambiguous standing in the human condition. The experiences were thought-provoking, salutary and often uncomfortable, but undoubtedly did nothing but good.

For this person-to-person encounter with myself I am more than content. For the way it was brought about I am grateful to my publishers and particularly so to my editor, Peter Evans, who always found a helpful response when I needed a target for my joys and fears.

I am also grateful to the people I met during the research, some of whom figure in the book but many of whom are recorded only in my memory.

I am beholden to my friends – John, Paul and Rita – for their co-operation and help. They served in more ways than they know.

Above all. I offer to my wife, Jill, my respect and loving admiration for the way she tackled our relationship during the making of this book. She listened and responded, sympathised and challenged, loved and hated me by turns, but stuck with me throughout the action. She was the constant focus for all my doubts and insecurities. She did not always understand what was happening but she was always ready to grapple with the actual and immediate, from the blind group gropes to the laying on of suspect hands. She led me to realise I had just that much more courage than I thought I had. For all of that, and more, she has my love and thanks.

I offer the book, in dedication, to my daughter, Sara-Jane, and my step-daughters, Fay and Jennifer, in the hope their generation will continue to relate person-to-person more kindly and effectively than mine.

D. B.
December 1972

INTRODUCTION

I approached this survey without qualm or anxiety because I was about to research an area of human relationships I thought I knew quite well.

And indeed, some of it I knew extremely well. After all, I had directed or observed many groups where the members were, voluntarily or otherwise, attempting to make new and deeper relationships with people they might or might not have met before. Let me add, they had not all come from the closed worlds of professional theatre or of amateur drama. There had been trade unionists; teachers — from tyro to sophisticate; college students — in and out of college; police and police cadets; public speakers, hotel receptionists; army officers; businessmen and priests.

My experiences with them had been, to use the jargon of the encounter movement, 'on-going' as well as 'marathon'. The range of personality traits, interpersonal relationships and sociodynamics had been wide; both sexes had been represented and the age spread was seventeen to seventy. My involvement had spanned nearly twenty-five years.

I was tempted to claim twenty-five years' experience. Now my research is completed, I know it would have been a false claim. I might perhaps be allowed one year's experience, twenty-five times over.

This is, however, hindsight. At the time I felt I knew the rules, ropes and roles pretty well. Nothing could have been farther from the truth. I was quite unprepared for the underground network of the person-to-person business where corridor gives on to corridor, door leads to door : corridors are unchartered and the doors work only one way.

All this I discovered, not merely by interview or observation, but by direct, personal involvement. To ensure a measure of objectivity I asked my family and friends to involve themselves similarly and I have had the benefit of their experiences as control factors.

My personal involvement was often facilitated by using personae, each created specially for the particular area to be researched. They had in common a pliable will and such run-of-the-mill opinions and attitudes that I often felt the persona to be neutered or non-existent. The need for this neutral pliability became obvious after meeting no more than my first two or three 'clients'; they were typical of the many who were content merely to *relate to me*, often obsessively so. There were few who wished *me to relate to them*. It seemed sensible to offer them the catalyst they sought. In this way they got what they wanted – and so did I.

With the exception of the incidents experienced by my friends in providing control factors, all the events recorded in this book actually happened to me and many memories, even a few scars, still remain.

Any reshaping or reshuffling has been motivated by clarity, discretion and, I sincerely hope, a sense of responsibility to the people and organisations with whom I came into touch.

In the interests of readability, I have written about only those things that seemed significant and illuminating. I spent much of the time involved in non-events with individuals and groups, but there seems little point in describing tedious exactitudes or trivia. The rest is reported as I experienced it – in the 'here and now'.

To protect the people I met, individually or in groups, the details have been deliberately disguised. People, places and incidents have been rearranged and transported, sometimes mixed, to give a sufficient and necessary guarantee of protective anonymity. Intimate involvements make specific personal revelations inappropriate.

In spite of the adopted personae, I found myself experiencing identity crises which left me drained and depressed for days – something new for me. It was not that I was no longer sure *who I was* but that I was unsure of my very existence. And not vaguely and metaphysically – I knew that brand – but directly and existentially. The role-playing, and the energy I used in prompting unique, direct responses from my companions burned more nervous energy than I had expected.

There was difficulty in relating normally to my family on

returning from some expeditions. It took longer than I anticipated to discard some of the personae. In addition was the very real misery that sometimes rubbed off on to me personally. Some memories are still very much with me.

Then there was the unexpected bonus of telephone calls where the caller hung-up no matter who answered our phone. For some weeks not a day would pass without ten or more.

During the same period I began to get posted circulars of a sexual nature – plain sealed envelopes, obvious in their uniformity. What intrigued me was not so much the nature of the contents, often enlightening and sometimes entertaining, but how the suppliers had obtained a name and address I had used to make an enquiry of an entirely different kind – supposedly in complete confidence. I put myself in the position of a lonely, middle-aged man, perhaps with a landlady or daily help. He could have been seriously embarrassed to receive similar post. Although many of the men I met were looking for easy and free sexual contact with one or more women, each was adamant he would not have liked such material appearing in the letter box. (One of the letters contained such a fascinating offer that I took it up. The results are reported later.) So much for all the guaranteed discretion and total confidence.

In spite of my best intentions, I sometimes got deeply involved at the personal level. Some relationships indeed resulted in my breaking cover. There was a recently widowed lady who needed to tell someone how much she had loved her husband. She felt he had died without knowing she loved him—in spite of their twenty-year marriage. It was a burden to her and she seemed unable to live with it, or to find anyone to confide in. I met her, contrary to my usual practice, more than once, and on each occasion she talked for more than three hours about her 'failure' (her word) with her husband.

There was an elderly man who could initially attract eligible ladies but, because of his personal habits, repelled them almost immediately. His habits were not distasteful, merely strange, and mainly of a financial nature. He found nothing remarkable in what he did, and never understood why the ladies did not meet him again. One peculiarity was his refusal to buy matches because they were 'too expensive'. He would accost strangers and ask for a match *or two*. Another peculiarity concerned his headgear. When out for the evening he always carried a large brown paper bag. Whenever it rained he would take off his hat, put it in the paper bag, take out a shabby cap and put it on.

I felt a genuine attachment to this quietly pleasant man and spent a number of evenings with him. One of his remarks skilfully cut me : 'I don't suppose you'll see me very much, anyway.' He was, of course, quite right. I tried more than once to discuss his peculiarities with him but had to admit to defeat. His mother had never complained – and he had lived with her for fifty-seven years.

The most rewarding personal experience has been the necessary re-examination of my own motivations in social and personal relationships, especially the intimate ones I had begun to think I understood. I am still wrestling with some of the new, but some of the old have withstood the burning.

I started the journey with what I hoped was an open mind. I now feel cynical despair for the manipulators and impatient sympathy for those manipulated. Both are in need of the same therapy. They are held by a fear of fear so strong that, forgetting they are also held in the human condition, they take useless weapons to an imaginary foe.

There is nothing to fear but fear and it is mainly fear that feeds the intimate personal confrontation business.

CONTACT

En passant

> Ships that pass in the night, and speak each other in passing,
> *Only a signal shown* and a distant voice in the darkness;
> So on the ocean of life we pass and speak one another,
> *Only a look and a voice;* then darkness again and silence.[1]

So wrote Henry Wadsworth Longfellow. It is one view of human encounters. Arnold Wesker has described another :

> . . . Jimmy says, we ought to start an association of them as need a bit now and then and we all ought to wear a badge, he say, and when you see a woman wearing a badge you know she need a bit too . . . and you say, how many lumps of sugar do you take in your tea? And if she say 'two' then you know she ent too badly off, but she's willin'. But if she say 'four' then you know she's in as bad a state as what you are, see?[2]

The two angles are not mutually exclusive – merely distanced by a century and the Atlantic – and their implications make up the substance of this book. Be it badge, signal or a look and a voice, the manifestation is neither novel nor recent – code words and secret signs being as old as the oldest profession.

The Christians' emblematical fish and the Freemason's symbolical digits span centuries. The self-selective esoteric group – the tribe within a tribe – has existed in most human societies.

In ancient China, privileged coteries practised contemplation, fire-eating and sexual unions with gross participation. Later, in Japan, members of equally envied fascicular groups pursued, en

[1] *Tales of a Wayside Inn*, Stewart, L. J., (ed.), III, 'The Theologian's Tale' (Dent 1921).
[2] *Roots* (Penguin Books Ltd 1959).

masse, intriguing pastimes with balls of metal and globes of glass.

In 1965, a hundred miles north of Sokoto in Northern Nigeria, I was permitted to stay with a tribe that regularly held secret 'group within group' meetings. My first discovery was that they were illegal and my second that they combined the 'old' (fertility-cult) religions with the 'new' (left-wing) politics. The groups were heterosexual and male dominated. Free congress (including male but excluding female homosexuality) was important and habitual at all meetings.

Coffee-and-wench houses were no more a feature of seventeenth-century England than they were of dynastic Egypt. Victorian London offered its well-known service of houses for gentlemen of landed leisure – houses more reminscent of camarillas than bordellos. New York matched it with a facility, of equal service but less fame, for ladies of distinction and discretion.

To-day, in London, Montreal and New York, sauna baths and encounter groups (to name but two) offer similar benefits. They are available to all sexes and their shibboleths are motley.

NEW FRIENDS AND OLD HABITS?

Motley may well be a key word in the person-to-person business. Certainly the coats worn by operators and clients are of many colours and there are many hats for different occasions. The contacts made may be described as 'New Friends' but many of them are new friends in old clothes. Old habits, of any kind, are not easily discarded.

There have always been symbols to signal sexual availability – homo or hetero – and there have always been meeting places for the unattached, temporarily or permanently. 'Greensleeves', the flower behind one ear and a particular manner of breaking bread are notable examples of other cultures' preliminaries to assignations. The instincts and their orderings stay the same, only the method changes.

Just as the motor car brought with it a major change in

national habits of adultery and fornication, and just as the package holiday (with or without organised camps and proscribed age ranges) heralded new ways of relating communally and socially, so the mushrooming of cheap printing and the use of the telephone have brought a major change in the habits of making personal contacts. Individual idiosyncracies in personal consummation remain as varied as the forms the human animal takes – it is the seeking and finding that have been embraced by the limbs of the media. Never before have so many spent so much in advertising so little.

Personal introductions, telephone numbers from small, black books and word-of-mouth are no longer exclusive agents. The twentieth-century esoteric person-to-person business has its entrepreneurs. The hippy, jet-setter, swinger, lonely heart or penny plain groupie in search of a suitable junto, clique or bunch will be aided and sometimes initiated by a buoyant near-industry using modern media.

THE PASSING SCENE

Sauna baths and encounter groups on both sides of the Atlantic are not the only organised group agencies affording opportunities for casual confrontations, for continuing liaisons or, indeed, for deeper relationships. There are groups especially for groupies (most eye-catching and well known amongst these being the nudist groups and the commercial necking and drinking parties – mainly attended by extrovert, self-confessed gregarious types); there are groups for doing (stamp collecting, crab collecting and graffiti collecting, fishing, gliding, hiking, dancing, singing – and photographing naked ladies); there are groups for making (painting, potting, working in wood – and one for polishing stones and banging iron bars into new shapes); there are groups for thinking (morals, politics, philosophy – about the beginning of the world and the end of it – concentration, contemplation, and many forms of the mystic and the occult, and even one group for thinking about thinking); there are groups for being (most are attached one way or another to the thinking groups but one presented itself with the legend 'Don't let it all hang out. Don't be a drop out. DROP IN and JUST BE').

The organised groups make up one of the happiest units in the person-to-person business. Motives of organisers and organised are exposed and there is a high level of customer satisfaction, validatable according to subjective and objective criteria. In all the groups I visited – and those under review were voluntary and self-supporting – motives of leaders and members coincided. They appeared to stem from what was, for them, a perfectly natural and normal preference to gather and socialise in groups that had the added bonus of a common interest : bonus, because for most of them it was the social and interpersonal relationships that topped their priorities – the vehicle being secondary and, while important, not crucial.

There was little vertical stratification in the relationships between leaders and led; little 'holier than thou'; little 'we are here to serve and help you'; little financial fleecing. Companionship and bonhomie were at a premium – as was value for money.

In these groups there seemed to be a high correlation between what was said and what was meant. Everyone seemed to be aware of their needs and wanted openly to satisfy them, rather than disguise and sublimate them. Everyone tended to be accepted at face value. There was no quizzing, searching for ulterior motives, scratching at the surface of personae or 'breaking'. Attendance at meetings was judged to be no more than a natural, sufficient and necessary manifestation of the human condition – accepted and enjoyed by all. Never once was I posed the favourite question of the encounter enthusiast 'but why are you here, *man*?' (How I was to get used to that, I hope, gratuitous description !)

Within the groups there was a tacit understanding that it was more fun to do things together – and even more fun if the interpersonal relationships were left unstrained. There was, for example, little pressure to :

conform to principles or practices any more than the actual situation seemed to require;

expose personal backgrounds and idiosyncracies;
become intense, enthusiastic or involved;
be unduly sensitive to the rigours of strict monogamy. (Most marital relationships were relaxed in the groups – with or apart from the spouse.)

There was an acceptance that doing, making, thinking and being were all aids to personal contact and to be pursued in a responsible and relaxed manner. Obsessive enthusiasts were tolerated – tolerated and no more. The groups were organised by voluntary bodies and this seemed to guarantee the absence of pressure to progress, learn or even become involved. The groups placed great importance upon self-development. In fact, they were outstanding examples of the Encounter Prophet's Prayer:

I do my thing, and you do your thing.
I am not in this world to live up to your expectations
And you are not in this world to live up to mine.
You are you and I am I,
And if by chance we find each other, it's beautiful.
If not, it can't be helped.[3]

It is extraordinary that the prayer should be met least pretentiously by apparently normal groups, doing normal things in a normal way and thereby enabling the frequent and rich celebration of the human condition through relating and interrelating, when the groups whose constant claim and aspiration that same prayer is fail to manifest or achieve it.

Relating in the group situation was the need of almost everyone attending and, since the need was real, dynamic and accepted, appropriate and successful techniques emerged. Given the need and a desire to satisfy it – to communicate rather than merely express – the techniques remain happily unexposed but none the less effective. Without the need, without the desire and with only the wish to expand and express the self, no matter the time, place, occasion or person, superficialities of technique take over and the spirit becomes lost or departs.

[3] Fritz Perls, *Great Therapy Verbatim* (California, Real People Press).

The techniques of relating without purpose and communicating without need were to be seen in dramatic relief in the professional side of the encounter movement. (Amateurs were more or less an extension of the egalitarian thinking and being groups with constant emphasis on free will and trust within each group — much more 'we're all in this together.')

Vertical relationships in rigid, structured (if unorthodox) group situations were the order of the day. Status reduction seemed the main strategy and hurtful rudeness the tactical secret weapon. Leaders were proud of their expertise, hesitant to cast off their mantles of mystique and commercially sensitive and successful. Motives of leaders and students coincided. Leaders wanted to help others achieve a better existential condition and students wanted to learn how to become leaders. For groups based firmly on the here and now there was great attention given to teleological ends.

There was little acceptance or confession of 'I am here because I need to be' — there were plenty of socially and morally acceptable reasons that adsolved the individual from personal need and responsibility. Needing people was at a premium however : not for a free-wheeling, voluntary, equal give-and-take relationship, but as a focus for the whims of personal experience and its expression — rather than agents for communication — and as targets to demonstrate each individual's ability to be arrogant, aggressive, hostile and rude and in particular as fencing partners on whom to improve the skills of interpersonal status reduction.

The main tenet of belief was 'I am intellectually and intuitively superior — and, what is more, I will prove it by my command of verbal and non-verbal techniques.' The main battle cry was 'You need me more than I need you. You may not know it, but that is only ignorance or self-delusion.'

The snake-eating-tail spirals of rationalisation made a mockery of the groups' expressed aims and principles. 'Know yourself and get deep in touch' was their emblem and shibboleth, but reflections and superficialities were all that were achieved.

Leaders and students alike were people who, in Wilde's phrase,

'Know the price of everything and the value of nothing.' They promised self-awareness, sensitivity, enrichment and, above all, getting into touch.

There was as little real personal contact, though more hostility, in the encounter movement as there was in the contact organisations themselves. Here the motives of organisers and members could clearly be differentiated. Some organisers were exclusively commercially minded and felt they were making a justified (though sometimes marginal) profit. A few, operating solo and with insufficient resources, must have been making a loss.

Generally speaking the organisers of the agencies – personal introduction brokers, pen club operators, get together promoters and marriage bureaux managers – combined some ideals of personal and public service with a wish to make a successful business of their work. Not unexpectedly, the more they stressed the service, the more woolly and ineffectual it was. The bigger the organisation the more respectable and reliable it tended to be, but this could never be a guarantee of worthwhile end products because of the nature of the clients. They needed the machine to be able to operate within those areas of social intercourse that are normally exclusively personal. Since this was the case, the agencies could hardly be blamed for a failure to relate within their clientele, who were self-confessedly not entirely efficient at making relationships. In this area clients get the service they ask for – to be put into touch with others who have also asked for help. The activity must, by definition, contain a high proportion of self-defeating mechanisms and manœuvres. Many of these agencies conduct their business through their own magazines.

They are however entirely different from those organisations who run the contact magazine industry itself. Here is a phenomenon of the person-to-person scene, where deception, in order to boost sales and consequent business as well as to avoid prosecution, is central to the system and in no way motivated by a wish not to offend personal feelings. (Delicacy of wording is a byword amongst some of the contact organisations. Most of it seems understandable and justified. After all, in resorting to an

agency to make companions or find a partner one is not likely
to welcome constant reminders of some of the more harsh and
ugly reasons for the application.) As will be seen later, it can
lead an unsuspecting customer into some potentially tense
situations, and for anyone who is not a practising swinger or
seeker out of professionals, the chance of 'overcoming loneliness'
(to use the euphemism of one mgazine almost entirely constituted
of call girls' advertisements) is more than remote.

The contact magazines conduct their operations in the country
of blind avarice where the one-eyed operator is king. He prints
the cards, shuffles, cuts, deals and plays according to rules he has
created: rules which sensitively reflect the needs of the times—a
groping of the middle-aged towards the sexual mobility of the
young. But a groping heavily overlaid with the trappings of
bourgeois puritanism. Satisfying sexual instincts yet guaranteeing
total cover up and keeping intact the pretences of rigid morality
is a suitable case for commercial exploitation.

The operators are more than prepared to provide the services
—at a price—for a clientele they openly despise and criticise.
Clients are more than prepared to pay for the tortuous cover
provided—at a price—while publicly criticising the phenomenon.
(It is only the extrovert professionals and the hooked swingers
who will speak at all frankly of their way of life—and they are
only prepared to talk to the converted.)

The ladies and gentlemen of escort and massage will hide
behind their improbable façades until the chips are down and it
is time to pay up and perform. They will leave open the door of
strict adherence to their advertised business until they are certain
of their catch and contact has been made.

Some of the magazines are run by operators who are sincerely
convinced they are preparing the way for a sexual revolution (in
fact, two editors I spoke to have been in the field for over twenty-
five years, although their cover in 1947 was deeper than it is
today. One of them said, illuminatingly, 'Just after the war they
all said I was a crank. Now they've put me on the wagon with
all the smut merchants.') Most operators confess to having found
an easy way of making a lot of money—provided they continue

printing their 'No Prostitutes' warnings and keep their copy ambiguous.

THE PERSONAL COLUMN

Stricter embargoes are placed on copy by *personal column* advertisement managers. What is acceptable as copy varies considerably from community to community and from advertisement manager to advertisement manager. In parochial, conservative areas it is possible to advertise for almost any kind of personal relationship if the language is ambiguous since strange and bizarre practices do not readily spring into the minds of their readers or proprietors. In more sophisticated communities advertisements are rejected out of hand if the content is sexual, or the wording at all in doubt.

(Even so, it is interesting to note what can slip through. The following might be straight from the pages of an adults only contact magazine. It is from the personal column of a local newspaper with a large circulation and an advertisement manager who believes himself to be 'up to all their tricks and a few more'.

> Lady would like to meet generous gentleman
> for occasional companionship.

I replied in a neutral but not unfriendly manner. I had not long to wait for her letter :

> Dear Derek,
>   Please ring the above number.
>   JUNE

She took the approach on the phone that it was difficult to write of personal things and better to talk. When I asked her to talk on the phone she said it was better in person.

I travelled forty-five miles to see her and within ten minutes it was established that although she was 'lonely because my husband has been dead for nine months' she was also 'prepared to lose myself in sex – it is my hobby' but not to lose herself so much that she would overlook her financial needs, which were £25 per visit.

The advertisement manager in question is still oblivious of the service he is providing in this particular instance.)

In contrast are the national underground papers, printing almost any copy, provided four-letter words are not too numerous. All kinds of relationships can be requested and spelled out. Ambiguities and euphemisms are not needed, the management seeming to apply little censorship. Male and female homosexuals, transvestites, little women wanting big men, white men wanting black girls, triolists, fetishists and groupies are all catered for.

The weeklies, with one exception, carry little more in their personal columns than details of educational courses – or, as we shall see later, encounter groups. The exception is a weekly advertising magazine with a large personal column made up almost entirely of people wanting to meet people. The range of opportunities offered to those looking for a sexual relationship – 'friendship first, possible marriage' – leaves little to the imagination.

It is difficult to gauge how much clients think of the results they obtain since few discuss their involvement, activities or motives, preferring to maintain an absolute silence. Those who *would* speak fell into polarised groups: those who had been swamped with replies and had found the results entirely satisfying; and those who had had no reply, or only one or two that later transpired not to be genuine. The subscribers' actions speak for themselves – the column fills many pages every week and its future seems as secure as its past.

The operators of the personal columns are convinced they are running an inexpensive service, wanted and needed by readers, in the public good. Although some that I spoke to seemed quick to make gratuitous judgments, most of them take what care they can, without being unduly repressive or uncommercial, to ensure they reject bogus or misleading copy. Readers who use the personal column, to advertise or reply, make up a microcosm of the person-to-person business, while proprietors occupy a middle position, not entirely commercial but business-like, with principles that are humane and rational if not the highest in human ideals.

In any one category there are charlatans, chauvinists, utopians and rogues : the whole spectrum of human aspiration and avarice is displayed. Nowhere better can it be seen than in the personal column – a phenomenon characteristic, peculiar and central to the whole business scene.

FRIENDSHIP GROUPS

Many of these were advertised in personal columns and some of the things advertised actually were susceptible of sensory perception. The irritation was, the things that were really interesting never occurred – only the dull and boring got off the ground.

There was a large selection : clubs for the old, the divorced, the separated, the crippled, elderly couples, alcoholics, neurotics and the plain lonely. However, the joys and pleasures they advertised in glowing abstract terms never achieved concrete, specific actuality. They were worse than being alone—so I was told and so I found for myself. The most frequent comments were : 'It's something to do', 'It's somewhere to go.' But no one said it might be better than staying at home by oneself. I quickly learned this etiquette : no one mentions the reality of their own loneliness or social inadequacy. Those who speak explicitly of their own condition are frowned upon.

Just as I had got used to this etiquette, I found myself involved in 'self-help' therapy groups operating on the edge of psychiatry, where it was a fetish to state one's own condition and to enquire about that of others. But in a strange kind of way this was just as impersonal, with everyone anaesthetised and depersonalised by apparently ruthless overfrankness. Alienation sets in (Brecht always referred to himself in the third person) and we, with a façade of frankness and rudeness, become 'third persons' – protected from engagement or sincerity.

The leaders of these groups were supposed to be specialists in the art of sensitive perception, yet they seldom pierced the externals of their clientele and the over-exposure of usually avoided subjects gave everyone another mask to use. (I was never once spotted as a writer in search of material. Every persona I adopted was accepted by groups and leaders alike. The search for truth and the techniques used to expose hypocritical façades that these groups claim as their forte, do not stand up well to examination.)

By invitation, I attended many functions where the gathering was small and depressing. The place was usually an upstairs room in a hotel and the leader either ex 1939–45 war type, still trying to be Air-Force-happy or, a lady of uncertain years begging everyone to be friendly while being entertained.

Entertained? More mesmerised. Whatever the content of the so-called entertainment the style was the same – quietly boring. 'Ken's slides', 'Bill's hike' and 'Jill's choice of cinema' were agony. The most off-putting feature was the atmosphere of doing good – the sepulchral air of helping others help you help them help themselves.

I persevered with some for three or four meetings and found the membership changed quickly, except for a central few. After only one or two meetings I saw I would soon become one of those chosen few, in spite of the dull and boring persona I had chosen for the occasions. I opted out, not unhappy to leave behind that world of organised, 'happy' socialising.

The friendship groups were all quite harmless. Except perhaps for those bigger groups advertising events which never appeared to happen. Unless, that is, I was too myopic to see the group when told 'You won't be able to miss us – we're all meeting outside the XYZ cinema and I shall be wearing a yellow maxi mac.' There were always plenty of reasons why events were cancelled or didn't happen and why I might have missed the meeting. I have spoken to three people who claimed to have been to at least one event. (The third person misled me by saying she had been – *it was really her friend who had been*. She believed her friend to have had a good time.)

...AND OTHER GROUPS

There were groups I was unsure about. These were the more esoteric groups and their members, from a twilight no-man's-land, spoke darkly of what they and their friends did at home or in their *other* groups. The cover-up routine of individual members was excellent. I was never able to trace with any ease anyone who did not wish to be exposed or pursued.

This phenomenon seemed to spring from the members themselves since the organisers always offered exactly what had been advertised. The events were anything from poetry to philosophy; from a seminar on violence to a weekend for amateur writers; from a group experiment in contemplation to a group experience in body massage.

(It was quite extraordinary how frequently massage cropped up. It was raised in philosophy groups, religious groups and encounter groups. In turn it led to Zen, health farms, nudism and a call girl circuit. In spite of society's apparent disapproval of 'body-touch', it came up constantly. Its disciples claim massage to be a non-sexual engagement. I found most people's involvement, if not their motivation, was erotic.)

In a less dramatic way I had come across many people, attending residential and non-residential courses, whose purpose seemed little connected with the subject of the course and who appeared to be there to involve other members in their special interests. Most of the courses were advertised as being creative and many were on theatre arts or closely allied areas. In this way they were just as self-selective as a nudist colony or an encounter group and in just the same way might be expected to throw up unorthodox students.

This self-selection towards a group that felt itself to be different (in so far as it was 'creative') might have produced more unlikely special interests than it did – many students attending with the express hope of making new, significant relationships. To this end, their special interests were made to work full time, but the range was limited: mainly palm reading, amateur psychiatry, tarot cards, seances, white-witch rituals (if the weather were clement) and other games bordering on extra-sensory perception.

On the one hand this can be justified by claiming the theatre to be a religious ritual and a spiritual force, therefore putting my suggestion into the realm of the improper. On the other hand I have seen too many students make immediate and overt sexual advances, and pursue them relentlessly throughout courses, not to conclude there are grounds to believe the educational course to be a *mere vehicle* for many members. Colleagues have drawn similar conclusions about much more academic courses.

The method of joining esoteric groups is simple. They advertise in the weeklies and many of them in the dailies. There are some who contribute regularly to those interesting guides—*What's on in Your Community*, or similar—for Britain and North America. All you have to do is to turn up. The irony is this: you are more likely to get a friendly, ease-making welcome at these groups than you are at one which sets out with the intention of being a friendly, friendship group. This is sad, in the first place since few who most feel the need of such a friendly welcome are likely to hear of the groups. In the second, they are more than likely to be put off by the idea of planting a seed in the garden of a Japanese tea-house or taking part in a discussion on the place of contemplation in modern domestic life. If some of the mystique could be dropped, many of the contact agencies would soon be out of business, since the rate of making personal contact in the esoteric groups is high, not only for disciples but also for chance guests. (It was fascinating, in one tea-house to find a six feet six, heavy-transport driver talking hard with a flower worshipping young man—about pollution.)

Not many esoteric groups have tea-rooms, cafés or open meeting places, but they are growing in number and strength. Good luck to them. Or, in their words perhaps: 'Peace and Sunshine.'

...'FRIENDLY'

The organisers of sexual, fraternising gatherings, sometimes simply called parties, varied from orthodox groups offering a service to prospective members by arranging informal events, to encounter-type groups' socials and fun-times (complete with humanistic dancing), to 'open', 'members and friends' and 'members only' clubs promoting Fun-times, Exhibitions and Adult Friendly Group Therapy. Many of them advertise openly.

There turned out to be more party-givers than I thought – and than most people I interviewed thought. The parties themselves are also more boring than most people expect. It was difficult to find anyone who had actually been to an orgy. Most people I spoke to thought there were few parties and that they all were a swinger's dream. In fact there are hundreds every evening but few achieve the distinction of developing anything more startling than alcohol, osculation and some under-garment fumbling.

Difficult as it was to find anyone who had been present at an advanced orgy, it was easy to find those who were interested in hearing and talking about them. I was frequently pressed for invitations to such events once it was established I knew something of them. The requests came more from men than from women but women were the more inquisitive. Imagination has a habit of surpassing achievement and when it comes to putting in an appearance at the parties, in spite of almost obsessive interest beforehand, there is a fall-off rate of at least 60 per cent.

Although most London cabbies were quite used to being asked for help in finding sexual partners (of either sex by either sex) not one of the forty-five I interviewed had been asked about parties, orgies or group sex. Cabbies in New York and Montreal responded differently, most being able to take me to an address or give me a number to phone.

From what I could discover, the only real orgies are run by the wealthy for the wealthy. I found them to be organised in well-guarded groups, protected from exposure by their network – a blanketing miasma of discretion and security.

Many of the party givers use contact men, false names, and accommodation addresses. The incidence of unlisted telephone numbers is very high. (Surprisingly, the Post Office's service[1] of giving a subscriber's name and address from a known exchange and number for the price of a three minute call is not widely known. It blows a hole in the defences of many individuals who wrote to me with an alias, from an accommodation address but with their real telephone number.)

[1] Now discontinued.

Most of the parties I attended were riddled with false laughter, pseudo gaiety and constant waiting for 'something special' to happen. Most organisers are on to a good thing financially and most clients are hoping for a quick erotic thrill. The little group sex that emerged was small consolation – for practitioner or voyeur – for the boring overtones of bourgeois cocktail parties. (The play on words was never suitably parodied or seized.)

...AND NOT SO FRIENDLY

Organisers and members of encounter groups had much in common. They all affected a lack of interest in money and in the standards of an acquisitive society – yet most were ready to give serious cosideration to the question of fees. (It was refreshing to meet the voluntary groups who compensated for their lack of sociodynamic expertise by a large measure of common or garden goodwill – a commodity much despised by the professional operators.) Pride was taken by the leaders in how much they charged and an equal pride was taken by members in the fees they had paid. The pride of all parties was symptomatic of the parading of self that seemed to motivate leaders and led.

My first impressions remain unchanged: the groups have excellent aims but wilfully refuse to live up to them or even try to put them into practice. Responses are not judged by standards of originality and genuineness, intensity and profundity, subtlety and rationality but by three tests alone: spontaneity, spectacle and sensation.

In contemporary society's state of deprived emotional education, many individuals sincerely and knowingly find themselves in need of outlets and modes of expression that are not easy to discover and therefore turn readily to groups who appear to speak to that condition. Instead of mature opportunities to open up dialogues of the soul through verbal and non-verbal techniques, optimistic newcomers are offered structures that are brash, naïve and superficial. But, like the party organisers, the encounter leaders are onto a good thing financially and keep themselves in

business by trading on the steady flow of members who are prepared to make the quick response rather than the right one and
who seem (some almost immediately and others after a time)
ready to pay hard cash for a quick emotional thrill. A seat at a
midnight thriller with a favourite enemy is a better bargain and
more in touch with the real world.

The groups that hold less extreme positions in the encounter
movement seem to have taken their techniques from drama
teachers in infant schools. They are certainly less harmful but
somewhat ill suited to help the 'well' get 'better' as so many of the
leaders claim.

Many members of groups said they joined initially in order
to make friends at meetings and also to learn how to make friends
better in their normal lives. They stayed on because they found
the meetings to be therapeutic, and *no longer* felt such a desperate
need to get into touch with other people.

There was no such maze of double-think about the clients of
the specific 'in touch' agencies.

CONTACT ORGANISATIONS

There can be no doubt that these agencies achieved much of
what they claimed in terms of putting people in touch with one
another and making contact. This external aim belied the real
motive of many clients – to be taught how to keep in touch once
contact had been made. Here it is that many agencies must stand
accused of misleading members for heavily and headily implying
that initial contact guaranteed freedom from loneliness for ever-
more. It is true that only a few actually made such a claim, but
most couched their publicity material in terms that clearly indi-
cated such prospects.

The contact organisations are different from the friendship
groups in so far as it is implicitly understood that members are
looking for partners of the opposite sex and not just any cure for
loneliness. They are different from the marriage bureaux touched
on later in that members are not necessarily searching for
marriage partners – though most of the women claim not to be

and *positively are*, and, strangely enough, most of the men claim they are and *positively are not*. Just one more example of the ironies that litter the person-to-person business.

Many of the organisations use computers, not only to give them speedy results in cross-referencing, but also to keep their image up to date. Many of them have managed to do this with great success and the traditional picture of a spinster of uncertain years, spinning romantic day-dreams around the lives of her pets, is no longer a valid one. The organisers are quite in touch with contemporary society and their motives and standards can easily and quickly be judged from their hand-out material. They see themselves as mounting a respectable service for those who are prepared to pay. They see their clients as individuals who would rather invest ready cash in an effort to get suited than waste time and money in meeting people through less unnatural social organisms. It is an attitude that appeals to organiser and client alike and is a suitable role for both parties to play, and there is some justice in it. There is more justice in assessing the agents as sensitive business people and their clients as rigid personalities who are not prepared to undergo the rigours of change required if they are to make more happy personal contacts than they have been able to do in the past.

This rigidity was clearest in the over twenty-fives. Younger clients made out good cases for the idea of dating strangers, with or without the aid of a computer, being an excitement in its own right. Those I interviewed used the agencies in addition to more usual methods of making contacts, not instead.

The contact organisations had something to offer at moderate expense and managed their affairs with less double-talk and more skill than the operators I shall talk about next.

CORRESPONDENCE CLUBS

I joined twenty pen clubs and wrote many, many letters. My details were supposed to be circulated not only throughout Great Britain, but over the whole world. I paid fees to clubs in England, the States, Germany and Japan. In each of my letters I enclosed a stamped addressed envelope (how well I came to know the phrase: SAE PLEASE) and one way or another spent a small fortune in trying to get in touch. From all my letters, stamps, envelopes, and circulated details, littering the globe I received *not a single reply.* It was not just a matter of waiting in patience — I waited eighteen months. I thought of others who had also parted with cash for the joy of receiving letters, waiting as I did, day by day and receiving nothing. It was, and still is, a sad thought.

MARRIAGE BUREAUX

No doubt there are bureaux working for the personal satisfaction of their clients and for the public good and no doubt more who believe they are. The scene consists of too many agencies making too many printed promises — most of which can never be realised. In particular, I received from too many bureaux too much material (mainly letters) purporting to be original, which, under examination, proved to be duplicated — some very well done, but duplicated nevertheless. My complaint is not against the duplication but against the duplicity. The failure rate may well be too high to carry the expense of personal replies, but the one petty deception suggests that other subterfuges may lurk. It is also an insult to a potential client's intelligence. I tried to discover how clients felt about this deception but their wish not to expose their connection with the marriage markets made it difficult to obtain much first-hand comment.

I happened to say to a friend : 'What do you think of marriage bureaux?' He looked startled for a few seconds and then smiled cynically. I found the response intriguing and asked many people the same question. Age seemed to govern their responses. Those over twenty reacted in exactly the same way as my friend. Later they would give more thought and offer comment but the immediate response was the same. Those under twenty said 'Don't know — never thought about it,' 'Don't know — what are they?' Their usual conclusion was that people who had to use them must be in a sorry state. This conclusion did not apply to the next group I looked at.....

CONTACT MAGAZINES

The picture became more unbelievable the more I looked at and into it. I uncovered an industry based almost totally upon the execution of sexual capriccios. At least, that was the first impression I obtained and that was the intention of the advertisers. It was not until I had become experienced (in language and manœuvres) that I found the realities of execution to be generally naïve and the capriccios mainly fantasy. (But only generally and and mainly – for any sceptics I can report, from personal experience, that there is hardly a whim, in or out of clinical casebook, that cannot be unearthed by patient foraging among the professionals of the contact magazines.)

It was a surprise to find *almost all the contacts were professional.* Many of them went to great lengths of disguise but in the end the 'little present' came up again and again. Two advertisements suggest the range:

> LADY late thirties, wishes to stock up (spirits) for Xmas; half bottle, half hour; full bottle, one hour. Help me have a very happy Christmas.   (Midlands)

> Firm but kindly male teacher experienced in early Victorian educational methods and skilful in their application seeks pupil of either sex who is genuinely in need of guidance.   (Middx)

Some of the magazines are available only on the underground market and some can be bought openly. There are some with a closed subscription list and some arrive through the post as a result of other contacts.

It was in the area of contact magazines that one of the major differences showed between Great Britain, Canada and the United States. In North America the contact magazines are far more detailed and explicit than those available in Britain. In New York they are sold on most street news stands for a quarter of the price that has to be paid in London – easier, cheaper and more comprehensive.

I found the proportion of genuine advertisements to be much higher in Canada and the States than in Britain. In Britain the proportion of non-professional advertisements can be as low as 5 per cent (in spite of the publishers' printed warnings regarding advertising prostitution) and in the States as high as 90 per cent. My research suggests the contact magazine has successfully taken over where the street prostitute left off, to become a rapidly growing, highly organised industry with rich profits for little risk and less labour. Indeed, close to this scene are the sex clubs with almost open doors. Most of the men involved are 'generous' amateurs, hoping to meet young nymphomaniacs. They do meet their young women, but they are not nymphomaniacs. Nor are they amateurs, merely business girls making their living as their talents best lie. Contact magazines, clubs and parties allow many girls, otherwise too unattractive to make a living on the open sex market, to come by an excellent source of income. Few men will travel fifty miles and decline at the last moment simply because their partner is not as attractive as they thought she might be. I came across many such women, attractive to their husbands no doubt, and many of them had one – often present but unseen when I made my contact in the matrimonial home – who would, however, have gained no second look, or other attenion, in the competitive situation of any High Street.

SEDUCTION, STUPRATION OR SHAMANISM?

Business girls, swingers with badges, personal masseuses, lonely hearts, personal columns or lumps of sugar – they are symptomatic of the need to belong, to identify, to recognise and be recognised. Code words and secret signs and understandings are as necessary to the person-to-person business as they ever were to Rosicrucianism. Indeed, throughout my research, I found striking resemblances to medieval witchcraft – almost a one-to-one relationship in ethos, preparation and event – with the exception of animal slaughter and cannibalism.

Consider the case of a young man or woman preparing to go to one of the parties or group meetings I have described. There is the *toilette*, the dressing and glamourising, the eating and drinking, music and dancing, consumption of drugs (nicotine and alcohol if no other), the games, rituals and sexual encounters.

Now consider the case of a medieval young man or woman preparing to go to a meeting of the local coven. Bathing and make-up, with perhaps a mask, would be a must. Then the 'massage' with oils of one, if not all the following: hemlock and aconite to toxicate the system and bring about strange movements, confusion, unusual heart and breathing action and slight dizziness; belladonna to produce an excitement which might grow into delirium; aconite and belladonna combined to affect the working of the heart and also bring about excitement. (None of these – and they all come from recipes for preparing the body to attend a sabbat – would bring about symptoms very different from those created by nicotine and alcohol.)

They would also use drugs to bring about heightened mental states. (Similar states to those sought by many yoga, contemplation and encounter enthusiasts, as well as those hoping for mystic illumination through the use of pot or LSD.)

There would be music, created by the group itself or by musicians specially imported. (True, it would be less technical than a peripatetic disco with its strobe lighting, but the manipulation by beat would be the same.) There would be dancing. Folk dances were still popular, performed in the ordinary clothes of the witches or in nudity, and there would be dances rather like the conga, palais glide and hands, knees and boomps-a-daisy. There would also be dances similar, generally and specifically, to the convolutions of rock, twist and reggae. There would be opportunities to eat rare and good foods (a bonus for them and just like dining out for us) and there would be no shortage of alcohol. When the time was right – when the coven, group or party was confident of its united identity – there might be the sacrifice of an animal. But there would certainly be sexual relationships, stimulated and/or protected by anonymity and/or promiscuity.

The structures underpinning the person-to-person business are also similar to those of medieval witch meetings : the use of special names; the convener known only to some; the unlisted telephone numbers and accommodation addresses (not wayside ditch holes but contemporary equivalents); the secret signs, codes and languages that speak only to the initiated.

The facts speak – with 'only a look and a voice' – for themselves.

A outrance

> To approach the stranger
> Is to invite the unexpected, release a new force,
> Or let the genie out of the bottle.
> It is to start a train of events
> Beyond your control.[4]

The rituals are many; the relationships are few. This book describes my journey on a road with few signposts, alongside companions with failing compasses. There was no public transport and a shared taxi costs more than money. When approaching the stranger it is better to walk; when inviting the unexpected it is better to be alone.

[4] T. S. Eliot, *The Cocktail Party* (Faber 1963).

GROUPIES

Come and Join us

ALL KINDS OF GROUPS

My attention was first drawn to the group thing by the following advertisement:

ALONE? — WHY BE LONELY?
Don't waste your weekends alone. Join great group just forming to spend weekends together.

I attended two meetings. The people, the atmosphere and the place were typical of many groups I met later: the separated, divorced, widowed, crippled, aged, alcoholic and neurotic.

We must have done other things but my memory is of sitting in a circle discussing our problems, or in a half circle looking at slides. I found the meetings pathetically sad, non-meetings really, because we never actually met one another. Barriers of excuses were walls between us, preventing us from relating. It was as if we were there to pass the time rather than get in touch. I *was* made at home. But home was for those with nowhere to go, rather than no one to go with. As such it left much to be desired.

I remember, more than anything, the overall atmosphere. A miasma of humility hung over us while we seemed to float on a lily-pad of hope on a pond of despair. All round was the world at large — a nightmare chorus of frogs. I wish I had happier memories — for my own sake and for those who paid their weekly 20p in search of the common touch. I attended too many similar meetings ever to see a notice like DIVORCED? without the sadness stirring.

MAKING THINGS

I found a different ethos as a result of following up this advertisement:

> Studio workshop community of people making things they love. Come and try it free for an evening – clay, firing, glazing, jewellery, etching, photography, wood and leather work. Its all for free but you pay for the coffee.

In spite of my incurable hamfistedness, I spent many happy evenings in the company of others who knew what they were doing. They seemed to get real pleasure from helping me. I tried many groups in the make/grow/eat your own thing scene. Some of them met once a week in converted garages and some had well-equipped premises in which they met frequently. Some had residential facilities and were glad to put me up for a night without charge. Some asked for nominal payment to cover twenty-four hours' hospitality and instruction. There was always so much happening that no one had time to consider who was lonely or not relating. It was taken for granted that people would get into touch with whoever they wanted, whenever they wanted. There was no need to create machinery to do it. Many were vegetarians, keen on some form of yoga-type physical exercise, and 'right into' one of the 'new' (or 'old') religions.

... AND WHAT IT LED TO

There were retreats, some free and some making nominal charges, and there were communes which from time to time welcomed guests. There were daily meetings of what I suppose must be called sects and there were evenings and weekends devoted to spiritual experiences. There were chapels and altars, soul-tanks and shrines; there was meditation and contemplation with lectures, libraries and tapes; there was the psychic, the mystic, the poet and the medium.

With most groups, friendship came *en passant*. No one appeared to be deliberately seeking or offering it. Their personal relationships were like virtue — 'given' as a result of something else and not under the direct control of the participants, and the overall atmosphere was of free-and-easy, give-and-take, relaxed relationships.

It is sad that the lonely people I met elsewhere stand little chance of discovering these groups and, in any case, would probably be put off by the esotericism.

RITUALS

In truth, some of the rituals I experienced were not for the shy or the unsure. At one I sat in a completely darkened room for well over an hour. We were in a circle and held hands. That is all we did — there was a rule of absolute stillness and silence. At another group I squatted for over two hours. At another I hummed in chorus; at another jumped about for twenty minutes and at another stood and then hopped on one leg. I also listened to many tongues and chants I did not understand. The most frequent ritual was taking off shoes and socks — an unhappy choice or necessity since for many it would be an off-putting embarrassment, although no one ever watched.

The rituals themselves took the place of friendship. For many the means had become an end — a place in the group was all they wanted or needed.

'TALK IT OVER'

I attended a number of groups that had an interesting technique. Everyone was known by a first-name-pseudonym. These groups were open to anyone who had a personal problem or, in their words, 'hang-up'. Their remedy was open discussion under the protective device of anonymity. Half the members seemed to be there to make a quick sexual connection — they were alive and lively. The others were the twilight/insipid type I had come to associate with self-help groups. There was nothing objectionable in the sexual overtures — the groups were insistent and considerate in avoiding personal intrusion – but the advances, made in and out of the formal sessions, seemed more important than anything.

The problems (or hang-ups) were similar to those played out at encounter group meetings but the discussions were wider ranging and turned to religion and politics in a philosophical style that would have been quite unacceptable to the here and now school. There was an emphasis on the rational that many other groups would have rejected immediately. It was frequently through apparent political debate that personal problems were aired.

Many claimed they found solace in being able to discuss their troubles in such a calm atmosphere. They felt the heated exchanges of emotionally based groups to be destructive. Not many had, in fact, been to encounter meetings, but all had heard of them and were equally critical. Their judgments were sound although based upon a strong element of fear.

The arrangements for meetings were, unfortunately, generally unreliable and haphazard but the members claimed the groups to be forces for good : 'there ought to be more of them', provided they were undertaken by voluntary bodies. In common with many groups they felt organised help or support, especially if it stemmed from governments, local or national, would defeat their purposes and kill their spirit.

NUDISM

At many group meetings nudism/naturism was mentioned. If women suffering from loneliness, inadequacy, or lack of contacts, could take the step to nudism they would find an almost instant remedy. Unhappily, the situation is not the same for men. Without a female companion a man will find it almost impossible to join any club or event as a temporary or permanent member.

I found the friendship and companionship factor high at nudist events, as was the incidence of relaxed sexual encounters. Certainly the atmosphere was informal and happy-go-lucky – none of the tense overtones I came across in other areas – and out of this informality came the opportunity for amiable overtures, as well as equally amiable but firm rejections. It was considered gratuitous and bad form to be intense about either advance or rejection.

Many of the contemplation and encounter enthusiasts were nudists and many nudists were inveterate party-goers. I received many invitations to cross the boundary of the particular group I was researching. Of those with a foot – naked or otherwise – in both camps, it was difficult not to draw the conclusion that what they wanted was a large circle of acquaintances rather than friends, and a groupie place in many bunches. There was a high degree of amiability and charm and no air of humility, mock or otherwise. The emphasis was on having a good time, getting on and getting off, and not on motives. There was no mention of problems, personal or otherwise. It was almost as wrong to have a problem in this group as it was *not* to have one in many of the others.

PARTIES

Since the boundaries were blurred and invitations frequent, the step to the party scene was a short one. There was plenty of choice.

> Come to Jack's Party – Paradise Cafe. Astrology – oil lamps – seances – improvisations – tarot cards – food drink and dance. Pay for the ticket – meet a friend.

> WEST END HOUSE PARTY – Are you bright, open and aware? Do you want to meet lots of interesting people in a friendly and warm atmosphere? If that's where you're at – this is where you'll want to be. Girls FREE till 10 p.m.

Some were extremely lively, happy affairs. The catering was good and there was plenty of decent wine. Only two turned out to be frauds – with professional hostesses.

One bring-a-bottle party turned out to be a swapping session for professional couples in the contact magazine business. I had

been invited in error, but fortunately no one made much of the
mistake and I was able to disappear without fuss.

Other parties were also business but a different aspect of it.
One of the agencies dealing in friendship and marriage gave
parties to introduce clients to one another. It was an excellent
idea. It would have been more excellent had we been told such
was the case. That is what I thought at the time – and so did
other chance males. In retrospect, it wasn't quite so bad as it
sounds, and I suppose the added excitement of the unexpected
guests made it more palatable.

IRONIES

Many of the coming-together rituals described in this chapter
belong to the area of tribal-anonymity or a search for a path in
life, rather than for a companion to walk it with. Most of the hip-
mystic groups seemed to achieve the sense of relating without
searching for it (and it was with them I was made to feel most
welcome and at ease).

Another irony emerged: those who seemed best able to relate
to one another were those who adamantly claimed there was
no hope of relating – total isolation being the human condition.
I would rather connect with them than those who accost at the
first opportunity with 'Relate with me, man', or 'I'd really like
to encounter you'. Relating and encountering were pseudo and
pallid by comparison with meeting young men and women who
helped me turn a piece of wood or showed me how to throw my
clay. We didn't 'need' one another. It was nice to get some help.
We didn't keep saying we needed one another. It was good to
give and take a smile and a quiet word.

I dwell on the memory of the quiet moments. I suggest the
reader does so too, since the rest of the book tends to be noisier
in almost every way.

ENCOUNTER
The Games People Play

AN ENCOUNTER WITH 'JOY'

I stood for a while outside the red-brick hall before making a move to the door. My wife waited patiently. I was hesitant on two counts: I felt old and drab compared with the adolescents who were rushing and pushing past; I had heard too many conflicting reports to be sure of what I was about to receive – except it would be a controversial, disturbing and uncomfortably direct 'here-and-now' experience.

I moved to the door, searching for the tickets that had arrived only that morning – a fortnight late. They were asymmetrical and an eighth of an inch thick with fluorescent green and orange figures. My wife had refused to have anything to do with them – saying they looked like psychedelic tarot cards. They certainly proved to be suitable omens for the event – a social, with the title 'come and joy'.

I searched for the tickets as we moved to the door. From behind, like smelly angels from a third rate hell, a new group pushed through the door, in spite of the keeper's best intentions, and carried us with them. They wore the strangest garb, with no shoes, socks or underclothes – the latter determined, not on close inspection, but at first glance. Their only cover: loosely fitting, flowing robes with holes in unusual places. The resultant display of sexual characteristics made it easy to tell men from women, otherwise it would have been difficult. The mens' heads were completely shaved, the women retaining half an inch of hair between skull and world at large. There were fourteen of them altogether – and that is exactly what they were: 'all together'. They moved in unison – it was almost sinister in its expertise – with apparently unmotivated and uncommunicated decisions. I saw a lot of them during the evening and they never lost their togetherness.

I went ahead, up the staircase, round the pillars and into the large hall where it was all to happen. The organisers had promised that our lives would be changed.

Inside, there was strobe lighting. Projectors threw images on the floor, walls and ceiling. There was a panatrope manned by a crew of five – hot and busy as Titans. In front of a bank of seven microphones was a gnome-like figure with long black hair, naked under a dark green monk's robe. He was hunched over one microphone like a dirt beetle over its muck-ball. His voice was extremely attractive : 'Your eyes are still closed and now you are being born.' There was a long pause. 'You are being born.' Another long pause. 'You are being born again.'

There were about four hundred people moving vaguely to atonal music. Some were still and all were lying on the floor – eyes closed, like the man said.

Or so it seemed at first. A closer look showed most people opening their eyes from time to time, mainly when they touched a new person and especially when a new person touched them. There was a discernible pattern : men opened their eyes when they made a new touch and women did so when they felt one. It seemed sexually motivated, a view supported by the average length of time couples stayed in touch. Although there was considerable variation in duration, the pattern was clear : the longest were heterosexual, the next were women together and the briefest were male to male. There were exceptions – some men obviously avoiding women and actively searching out men – but the norm was men passing one another with minimum touch and little response. It proceeded by common consent.

After the joys and challenges of birth the leader, describing a brave new world said, 'Be anything you want to be. Do anything you want to do.' For some this meant a radical change and more than a few immediately made animal noises, some loud and weird, some delicately beautiful. For most it meant continuing or developing the process of being born.

After a while the music abruptly stopped and changed to brief extracts. (The Titans may have had problems in finding the right record since one extract eventually continued uninterrupted.) The music was loud. It became very loud and, whatever the intention, the atmosphere was dramatically altered.

Most of the time the leader used his voice beautifully and well, but during the next half-hour he had to fight a continual battle with the panatrope operators. At times the music was so loud he had to shout into his battery of microphones. Sometimes he was left shouting over silence, as if the stylus had been lifted from the record. Many found this frustrating, but some accepted it happily.

The leader organised what he called a 'creative dance of freedom' but for those who needed help or encouragement there was a progression of suggestions. 'Dance with your fingers and hands – dance with your feet and legs – dance with jerky movements – dance with smooth movements – dance with at least two other people – dance with your shoulders, your bottoms, your spines – now dance with someone else's spine – now dance in two large groups – now dance in one large group with everybody together – and do it with your eyes closed.' This last instruction was obeyed immediately and there was a consequent mass (mess) of falling bodies. This achieved much affectionate togetherness with a high level of giggling and shouting.

We were told to take our group dance down to the floor and 'grow together'. This triggered off much touching. It was busy and inaccurate at first but shortly settled down to a quieter rhythm. I was able to watch the 'touching' dance at close quarters. I was in a position where observing was easy and there was no embargo on watching or opting out, for which I gave the organisers full marks. I found a battle of wills (and bodies) going on at my feet. A young woman and an older man were stroking each other's heads with quiet absorption. It was a pleasing sight and I watched with empathy.

Slowly and almost imperceptibly the man's hands moved away from the girl's head to more obviously sexual areas. With light stroking movements he touched her lips and neck with one hand. With the other he more firmly massaged her breasts and pelvic area. The girl seemed to enjoy it and the man interpreted her signs of pleasure as an invitation to proceed to further intimacies. The next ten minutes were occupied with a struggle between the man and the girl. The physical manifestations were slight but the battle of wills was intense. Whenever the man touched bare flesh, no matter where, apart from her face, the girl put out rejection symptoms. It was some time before she used her hands to repulse him but she expressed her feelings clearly by making sounds (not words) and twisting her body. It was strange that after each of these rejections she warmly welcomed caresses on breasts and pelvic area, appearing to get more and more satisfaction on each occasion. It seemed she would have been pleased by massage to orgasm, but only if 'protected' by her clothing. The man was not satisfied with this, lost interest after the ten minute struggle and went passive. The girl tried once or twice to guide his hands back to her breasts, but he was not prepared to play.

During this confrontation both girl and man had their eyes firmly closed. The man was quite relaxed, but the girl's nervous tension was shown by the tense flickering of her eyelids. They drifted apart and were absorbed in larger groups and by this time there was a fair amount of explicit sexual touching and stroking. How it might have developed must be left to the imagination. The leader declared a coffee break.

During the break I made attempts to contact singles and couples, as did my wife. We both found little enthusiasm for a friendly 'Hello', and after a dozen overtures to the clientele, we turned our attention to the refreshment and cloakroom staff. It was with welcome relief that we found we were not afflicted by spiritual BO. But it was sad that the most friendly and approachable people were not involved in the encounter social. The staff were all interested in the event which they found weird. One middle-aged, attractive coffee lady's reply to 'Would you like to join us?' was predictable : 'What do you think I am – mad?'

I left her to catch a trio of young women who were just about to depart. I had noticed earlier their lack of commitment – one of them had been hostile and vocal. They were more approachable than those who were staying. I noted the irony. Two of them had considerable experience of encounter groups and felt the evening to be a travesty. The third had come at their invitation. All three were disenchanted and told me with great relish they had just succeeded in getting their ticket money refunded. They described in lucid and articulate terms the joys and benefits of proper groups. They were even more lucid about the 'charlatans' who were running the social.

(I met them later, on the way home. They were much happier having had a meal at a nearby Chinese restaurant. They gave me details of their encounter group and told me I would receive a welcome that would more than compensate for what had happened during the social. Unfortunately I was never able to take up their offer.)

Just before the coffee break ended I was approached by another attendant who obviously wanted to chat. He battened on to my wife, quizzing her as to why 'such an attractive and *normal* woman should want to be involved with all this'. Without waiting for an answer he began the story of his life: he said he was a part-time steeple-jack and tight-rope walker, but was interrupted by the leader urging us all to the next stage of the proceedings.

We sat on the floor in a circle and a presentable and lithe young man talked to us from the centre of it. He said he was going to 'abstract the essence from the sounds, the lights, the atmosphere and *anything you all might offer*[1] as a stimulus for free, dramatic dance'. He would 'spontaneously perform' in front of our very eyes.

Having explained it to us three times he stood quite still, apparently waiting for something to happen. The lights were functioning but there seemed to be trouble with the music. After a minute or two one member of the group came to the rescue, or so I thought, by making an intriguing and dramatic noise in the back of his throat. It was a genuine piece of participation and a good stimulus for spontaneous dance. The young performer refused to respond. One or two more joined in with the throat noises until the challenge lay in the hall like a solid edifice. Fortunately for the dancer the music came to his rescue.

[1] My italics.

In his defence it must be said he danced rather well in a pseudo Martha Graem style, but for me the event had been killed by his wilful refusal to execute what he had been at such lengths to describe. The solo part of the performance did not last for long. He soon approached a girl in the audience – for that is what it had become – with an invitation to dance. The invitation was in the form of extended hand and arm waving, finally leading to hand clasping and the girl being almost dragged into the arena – for that is what the space had become. For a moment it seemed as if we were going to witness ritualistic rape, until, apparently apropos of nothing at all, the girl was left in the circle and the dancer fetched another. She was the same size, shape and colour type as the first. The pattern was repeated with five more – all the same physical type.

The last one had the young man matched from the moment he approached her. She was as good a dancer as he was, slightly more agile and of equal will and energy. He failed to overcome her in dance, and tried direct physical contact. This failed also, since she was his equal there.

By this time there was a move towards total audience involvement. The green robed monk leader had made one or two suggestions to men on the outside of the circle and they had joined in. The failure of the dancer to subdue the girl was no longer exclusively on show and he tried to retreat. The girl had him by the foot and he couldn't. Finally she took him to the end of the room, deposited him in a heap and walked triumphantly away.

I spoke with her a few minutes later. In a broad Irish brogue she said he was a phony, making excuses to philander with girls he found attractive and she wanted to take him down a peg or two. I told her I thought she had done more than that. She replied 'I'd only just started.' Since she was dressed in black leather trousers, boots with matching belts and bracelets, with the sign of the swastika clearly on her breasts, I took her word for it.

That seemed a fitting moment to leave the event – bodies were down to floor level again for more groping. By now there were fewer inhibitions. It promised to become a groupie paradise of eternal groping. There was a high level of enjoyment, absorption and even some consideration for other people's wishes. For most people it seemed a good return for the evening's investment. For my wife, only the background music made it a different experience from the rush hour tube. So ended 'Come and Joy'.

Others may have had peak experiences, but they were denied to us. We felt little different after than before – certainly no better – and we were intended to, for the claim most frequently made for such group activities goes : 'As sick people get well – so well people get better.'

Perhaps my wife and I were neither sick nor well – just used to living in our skins. This too is a favourite encounter question : 'Are you happy in your skin?' To claim we were is perhaps to be smug, self-satisfied and condescending.

AIMS AND CLAIMS

'Skin-happy' and 'getting better' are phrases from the jargon of the encounter movement. There are many others : 'nurturant', 'being in touch with your feelings' and 'finding out where you're at', but they have little place here.

In plain language the movement has splendid aims : to deepen the sense of self-awareness; to bring about sensitive and compassionate understanding of others; to create personal and social responses, as flexible as they are honest; to foster personal growth and to do so within a society that is creating its own identity. The following speak for themselves :

From Esalen Programs

ESALEN : A STATEMENT TOWARDS CLARIFICATION

Esalen has come to be thought of in a number of ways – in so many, in fact that we sometimes speak of ourselves as 'Inkblot Institute'. Among these projected 'identities' and our relation to them, are :

A *sensitivity training* center. This is a term we rarely, if ever have used. That increased sensitivity is a hoped-for outcome in many programs is of course true.

A growth center. We recognise that the 'growth center move-ment' has largely developed in relation to Esalen. We still best consider ourselves to be an evolving kind of school for experimental education and not a place that can, in any sense, promise a particular result.

A psychiatric hospital. On one occasion the Miami police called asking if a person then in their custody had 'escaped' from our 'institution'. We are not a hospital and do not give the type of 'care' or 'treatment' identified with one. Our programs are oriented toward growth rather than pathology and we believe explicitly so. The stament made in relation to Gestalt Workshops is applicable to all programs : 'The assumption is made that participants are not "patients" but are persons responsible for their own life decisions.' Anyone not willing to make such an assumption about him-self should find resources other than those we presently offer.

Particular Identifications with one or another of the areas of work in which we have been involved such as encounter or Gestalt or sensory awakening or structural integration. Here our function has been to facilitate the development of work in those and other areas but we are not solely involved in only one or two of them.

A religious center or retreat. This is true to the extent that an individual chooses to make it so. Historically, Esalen began largely out of the founders' interest in Eastern philosophy and spiritual practice and part of the program remains focussed in those areas.

From The London School of Personal Growth
THE LONDON SCHOOL OF PERSONAL GROWTH
A Higher Education Centre for Men and Women of Any Age.

PURPOSES
To help achieve bodymind release, integration, health and development;
To help solve personal and interpersonal problems.

METHODS

1. *Demonstration-Talk-Discussions*

To discuss in a non-dogmatic, non-authoritarian spirit the theory of a family of methods including psychoanalysis, psychotherapy, Gestalt therapy, neo-Reichian bionergetics, intensive courses, psychodrama, relaxation massage, shiatsu, mutual hypnotism, yoga and meditation.

2. *Group Sessions*

(a) One-Time Encounters.

    To bring people together in non-verbal and verbal interaction, to increase awareness of scope for growth.

(b) Weekend and All-Day Encounter Workshops

    To introduce special methods, such as bioenergetic energising exercises, controlled release, Gestalt, psychodramas, marathon encounter, Esalen massage and shiatsu.

(c) On going Weekly Two-Hour Encounter Group Sessions.

    For men and women (including couples) to help them to be more spontaneous and honest in verbal and non-verbal interaction, to recognise and acknowledge how they contribute to their own difficulties, to deal with personal and interpersonal problems, and to release locked feelings and energy in order to foster bodymind health and growth.

(d) On going Weekly Two-Hour Verbal Group Sessions.

    With the same purpose as on going encounter groups, but without special emphasis on non-verbal methods.

3. *Individual Sessions*

(a) 50-Minute Verbal and Non-Verbal Sessions.

    To deal with specific problems, such as psychosomatic inhibition, anxiety, depression, phobias, migraine, impotence, frigidity, repetitive breaking off of relationships, self-destructive or self-defeating patterns of behaviour, or non-specific malaise, the lack of bodymind well-being, zest or exuberance, the restriction of

life-style through fear or suppression of strong feeling.
The method used is educational, not medical.

(b) 50-Minute Bioenergetic Massage and Energy Release
Sessions.

With a similar purpose, but with mainly non-verbal
methods.

(c) Intensive Courses (Emotional Release and Re-education).
To break down defences which maintain a self-defeating
pattern of behaviour, feeling and attitudes.

The course lasts three weeks, during which the student
must be completely free of all work, family or social
obligations.

The names of some of the organisations are also of interest . . .

SELF Institute; VIDA (Ventures in Developing Awareness);
PNP (People Not Psychiatry); OASIS; PEOPLE; DIIPF; SYNERGIA;
DYNACOM; QUEST; YOLOT; Interface Inc.; WILL (Workshop for
Living-Learning).

. . . as are their advertisements . . .

'Females needed to balance up free encounter group.'
'Encounter Group for the enterprising but responsible.'
'Weekend residential course exploring Human Contact.'
'Communal living residential workshop.'
'Psychoanalytically-orientated group teaches how to counter
inhibition, anxiety and depression.'

I found the question of advertising of interest. At the end of
the chapter is the story of my struggles with the press to get
published what I thought at the time to be innocuous copy. I
was to find the encounter movement, and its advertisements,
were viewed with suspicion by advertisement managers.

Some of the titles of events stimulate mind-boggling possi-
bilities. In her book *Please Touch* Jane Howard tells of an
invitation she received to an encounter meeting for those
with prehensile toes. Here are a few of the delights I came
across :

5 DAY EXPERIENCE

A five day pot pouri [sic] of experiencing. The leaders describe it as a workshop playground for people who want to find ways of getting high without drugs. We will show you some of the trips we know, venturing into different worlds each of the five days.

HALLOWEEN RITUAL MAGIC AND FANTASY — CHRISTMAS MASSAGE

SUN RISE — BREATHING AND AWARENESS — EXPLORING MADNESS — HOW TO BEAT THE GAME — PANTHEISTIC AWARENESS AND BIOELECTRIC FIELD EFFECTS — SOMATIC WHOLENESS — THE ALCHEMY OF SCHIZOPHRENIA — ON BEING A WOMAN — RISK APPROACH TO BEHAVIOUR CHANGE — PERSONAL FEEDBACK METHODS — MODELLING AND ROLE PLAYING — BEYOND THE LIMITS OF SELF-LIMITATION — BEYOND GAMES . . . JOY THROUGH AWARENESS — INTERPERSONAL SPONTANEITY VS THE FALLACY OF 'TRYING TO RELATE BETTER' — THE I-THOU TRANSCENDENTAL INTEGRATION METHOD OF SELF-ACTUALISING — HUMANISTIC DANCING — ANGER AND WHAT TO DO WITH IT !

Interesting as this background may be it has the drawback of suggesting the existence of a dynamic ethos and *modus vivendi*. I found this to be untrue. I also found untrue the stories of nude orgies, sex parties, hysteria and fatal collapse. There were isolated incidents of some of these, but had I been in search of that kind of sensation, I should have been sadly disappointed. Much more central was my experience of a group for beginners.

INITIATION

As a first step, I rang the organiser :

'It's a bit difficult to describe, but we have lonely people who are pretty fresh to the whole thing and so we . . . we just . . . mmm (laughs) relate with other people. It's mainly just fun.

'Our groups are mainly sort of drifting towards opening up people emotionally — you know, sort of sensitivity training groups. I must explain we're all working completely voluntarily it's just myself and my friend who've had some training in this.

'Couple of weeks ago we got one guy who was so nervous that he was trying to work it out in a very sexual way and we simply tell every new person that if anyone tries to lay anything heavy on them to say a very big "no". . . . There's another group on Sunday which has been going a year. And we've got to know each other so well that occasionally we'll have no clothes on and this sort of thing. Just being able to feel happy – just being able to live in your body. It begins at eight o'clock to give people a chance to get from work. If you like to come an hour earlier, *have some coffee and get to know people*,[1] that's fine.

'Most people are pretty frightened so you mustn't worry.'

As it happened there was little coffee drinking and even less getting to know people. I arrived at seven thirty and was shown into a small room adjoining the kitchen of a fairly large flat. The shabbiness of the room was disguised by a display of wall posters. Three people were already there; the atmosphere was apprehensive. After twenty minutes of stillness and silence we went into a bare upstairs room. We were invited to take off our shoes and socks, being told it was a rule. We were gently instructed to spread out, find a space and lie down. So far it was like a primary school drama class.

The connection with primary schools went further: after some initial relaxation exercises with legs in the air and much noise-making we were told to be babies – lying in prams, laughing, gurgling, crying, screaming, wanting food and not wanting food, wanting to be loved and not wanting to be loved. The last exercise was 'cry for mummy'. Mummy did not come, so baby had to console itself.

After the self-consolation we were told to find a partner to play with – the emphasis to be on body contact, mainly with hands, feet and 'eye-to-eye' contact. The whole of the exercise, we were told, was to be non-sexual. This grew into playing with

[1] My italics.

one another's faces – pulling, pushing and poking, to 'get as much fun as possible'. It developed good relationships for a lot of people and grew quite naturally into 'partner comfort' and soothing.

We were then organised, with eyes closed, into a full group lying in the middle of the room. There was touching, stroking, sniffing and groping. We then grew upwards, first on to all fours and finally into a standing position. We were then supposed, spontaneously, to sway and hum in unison. At this, one of the girls burst into tears. It had begun as a slow sob which was barely distinguishable from the humming. By the time the leaders noticed it, it had grown into deep crying. She was hugged by one or two of the women in the group and then led out. We didn't see the girl again that evening.

My partner was next chosen for special treatment. She was placed in the middle of a circle made by the rest of us and thrown, gently but thrown nevertheless, around and across the circle. During this she kept her feet firmly in one spot. This seemed to have the desired result for we were then told we could move on to an exercise not permitted if the group was not working well. My partner was then lifted and carried by the group. She was rocked, swayed and lifted up and down. The intention of the exercise was to relax her, and the leader was displeased that she had not felt relaxed.

After this came a total change. We sat in a circle. We were invited to go into the centre individually, and tell the group what was worrying us. The first was an elderly man and the second a young girl. They seemed to have nothing worrying them except telling the group what was worrying them. We spent a long time discussing the problem of standing in a circle telling strangers about your problem of standing in a circle telling strangers. . . .

The third volunteer was a different case. For him it was an opportunity to demonstrate his skill as an amateur psychiatrist. He told us all, individually and at length, what was wrong with us. He saw himself as analyst and mystic. Not unexpectedly this evoked hostile reactions. They were cleverly filtered off by the leader who got the young man to play the part of an unwanted dog, while the rest of us threw cushions at him. This cushion throwing relieved feelings, became fun for everyone and, a nasty 'encounter' having been avoided, we went downstairs for something to eat.

The atmosphere at the end was more friendly than at the beginning, but still at a level of avoidance rather than acceptance. We left quietly in ones and twos. It had been very much in the nature of a non-event. No one had related with anyone they did not know before and neither my partner nor I had managed to make a new contact.

CONFIRMATION

This absence of relating and making contact did not apply to another group meeting I attended. It was advertised as intensive. The surroundings were attractive and the atmosphere lively. There were fifteen in the group, five men and ten women. The average age was thirty – ten years older than the previous group.

We started with an eyes-closed-touch-up-group-grope (or 'non-sight-orientated-in-depth-tactile-exploration'). We followed with trust exercises (being thrown around) and followed that by forming a circle with one in the middle to talk. We talked of our homes and jobs, our hopes and fears, our friends, our enemies and our dreams. The pattern was familiar and not at all intensive.

Just before lunch, Janice, a young Scots girl, spoke for the first time. We had started at ten and it was now twelve thirty. She told us she was afraid of being touched and was always an outsider. This gave the leader a chance to promote action. We were told to form a circle and to exclude Janice. This we did. Janice tried to join in – first by quietly asking and, when this failed, by gently touching. (I have never met anyone whose touch was so non-tactile.) Of course, none of this succeeded. The exercise began to bite.

At first it seemed no more than a routine exercise that Janice felt obliged to undertake to please the leader. As it progressed it grew in meaning for her, and her failure to join the circle took her to screaming panic. Some members of the group weakened and let Janice in. This brought a flood of tears from her, guilt from us and complimentary noises from the leader, whose sense of dramatic timing had no doubt brought us to such a point, just in time to eat. With a vague feeling we had achieved something meaningful, we went to lunch.

It was an informal, friendly affair and we appeared to be *meeting for the first time*. All the ideas, attitudes and opinions we had learned during the morning session might never have existed. It was my first insight into the *failure of carry-over* that I was often to find in the return to reality after encounter meetings.

After lunch there was more general chat – who was who and what was what. This turned into group discussion on what to do next. Unexpectedly this led, not to a decision, but to more action. One of the young men, Len, blurted out he couldn't get on with his father. Previously he had been quiet, taking a supportive rather than an active role. He was given the floor and with splendid language flow, talked about his poor relationship with his father. He spoke at length and would have continued had he not been interrupted by one of the older men turning to the leader and saying, 'You know me. I'm Duke. I can break him – if you'll let me. Will you let me break him? Will you?' The leader gave her permission and we watched Duke, a solidly built six footer, walk slowly across the room to the frail figure of Len. He stood for a good minute face-to-face with his arm raised as if to strike. He appeared to be merely threatening. Not so! Duke rained a series of punches at Len's shoulders and kidney areas – strong, hard-hitting punches. Len did not move, not even the proverbial eyelid. Not until Duke stopped. Then he wept, first by himself and then on Duke's shoulder. Duke held him for a time. Then he turned to the leader, 'I said I could break him, didn't I?' and eased Len, who was still crying, down to the floor. Duke walked back to his place.

Anne, a strikingly beautiful girl, kept her eyes fixed on Duke as he walked across the room. Then she spoke out. What she said followed logically from Len's case. She couldn't relate properly with her father – but her idea of relating properly was unexpected. She wanted her father to seduce her, or rather attempt to do so and be unsuccessful. She would then successfully seduce him, or rather he would respond fully and Anne would fight him off. The ultimate would be her father's loss of control and her loss of virginity by rape. We were allowed no time to consider or discuss Anne's problem. The leader immediately asked: 'Is there anyone here who reminds you of your father?' A pause, then, 'Yes, there is, Duke.'

Duke was already on his feet and making his way to an apparently petrified Anne. The rest of us were gripped by a sense of inevitability and watched Duke set about the task of being whatever he thought Anne wanted or needed of her father. It was a strange, tense fifteen minute experience. First there was the physical struggle to get Anne into the arena. Duke finally carried her there. Then there were Anne's attempts to escape, all easily foiled by Duke's strength and speed. After this the real struggle set in. Duke started by trying to kiss her. Since it was not difficult for Anne to prevent this he changed his approach. His hands went to her breasts – from the front, from behind, from above and below – and whenever Anne defended that area he switched to her crotch. Wherever Anne put her hands she missed. It was through his skill and split second timing that Duke achieved real ascendancy and Anne became genuinely defensive. Before, although showing some anxiety, Anne had appeared to treat it as a game. Once Duke was able to handle her breasts and crotch at will, she was no longer sure how much of a game it was.

From the onlookers' point of view it was certainly no game. Duke's pants gave evidence of an erection. Anne began to make submissive movements and noises, but Duke would not let the confrontation end. The struggle entered its last stage. Anne no longer avoided his hands but tried to dissuade him by words. This merely encouraged Duke, and in no time Anne was on the floor in her underclothes only – Duke had flung her skirt away. Her blouse was ripped in two places. Duke sat on her pelvis and, ignoring her pleading, ordered her to take off her bra. There was no further physical exchange, except Anne was pinned to the floor. She refused. 'Don't you talk to me like that' –

'I'll talk to you any way I want – and you know it.' Duke had won. Anne sat up and took off her bra. She had submitted completely and relaxed into the sensuality of the situation, appearing to have forgotten about the rest of us.

Poor Anne. No sooner had she submitted than Duke was back in his seat – Anne left to look pathetic in the middle of the circle. She was not left for long. Three events occurred almost simultaneously. An older lady, who had earlier shown signs of being attracted to Duke, harangued him for his performance. Janice, with Carla, an older American girl, went to Anne, helped her to her feet and took her to a corner. They stayed there for some time and claimed in later discussion to have held a group confessional, discovering latent Lesbian tendencies. Although none of us had noticed it, they said there had been kissing and caressing in the corner.

Most attention was given to Len who had been led into the circle by Ruth, a middle-aged housewife from H. E. Bates. They stood for at least five minutes in a close embrace – quite, quite still. Duke's antagonist had calmed down and the trio in the corner were overlooked. It appeared that nothing more would happen. The leader declared a coffee break.

Once more there was no discussion of the events in the 'other room'. It was as if that world ceased to exist the moment we left the room. When we returned there was rapid cross-fire discussion about the events of the afternoon and this, together with some well-timed relaxation exercises, took up the rest of our intensive encounter.

Try as I may, I cannot place the people I met in that room in another life situation. They exist only in the interpersonal relationships of that group. I searched out, Len, Anne, Duke and Janice. I spent a lot of time with all four, but we were never able to relate in the same way as we had before. It is revealing that although all of them vouched for my report exactly as it is written *for the others* – each denied their own part. It was as if they had dreamed their own selves away and lived only the lives of others. Revealing, since one of the main purposes of encounter is to get more in touch with one's own feelings, and others', in real terms.

COMMUNION

There was nothing unreal about the following session. It was what it claimed to be from beginning to end – a massage group, and once etymological misunderstanding had been removed from my mind there was no ambiguity. Massage had always been for me an exact term denoting a physical activity, probably athletic, and with no suggestion of theosophy-person-to-person-psychic-relationships. The massage was mystical in purpose and caressive in technique.

I arrived to find a group of men and women, average age twenty-five, in yoga-like postures. There was one Lotus position being correctly executed. It transpired that most of the group had previous massage experience.

We began with an introductory lecture. This was followed by a 'pig-in-the-middle' circle. We were asked to say who we were, what we were, why we were there, what we had done before and what we were hoping for. Everyone was sympathetic and no one was given a rough ride – different from some other groups where everything, even one's name, found a hostile disbeliever. But here, amicability was to be the keynote for the day. We were a mixed group. The age range was nineteen to sixty-two and we came from Canada, the States, Australia, Russia and Great Britain. Some were single, some married and some living together, one pair and one trio.

The first exercise was deep breathing. To prepare for it we took off all jewellery, rings, watches etc. For over a quarter of an hour we sat with legs crossed and mouths open; breathing – 'sensing the flow of energy into all the separate parts of the body'. Many people claimed to succeed in unlikely extremities. I wasn't sure how energy flow to my left thigh should feel, but after sitting with eyes closed, breathing deeply and listening to the leader's pleasant voice for a quarter of an hour, I began to enjoy the experience, even if in a state of mild hypnosis.

After this we reformed the circle. The leader went into the middle, took off all her clothes and invited another girl to do the same. This happened without fuss or comment. The men found it intriguing and erotic. (It came out in private discussion later, that some of the men had been hoping for such an event.) The leader gave a demonstration massage. It lasted for over an hour and, against my expectations, kept the whole group interested. The massage itself was a combination of smoothing, stroking and caressing, undertaken with maximum body-to-body contact and helped by the use of oils. The leader used a 'drawing out' technique to release energy, capture it and discard it. I was able to accept this only symbolically, but some were convinced it *actually happened*. The leader obviously enjoyed her work and the demonstration. The candidate spoke convincingly of her enjoyment, relaxation and feeling of goodwill, especially to the leader.

Then it was our turn. We were asked to find a partner we would *like* to work with, take off as many clothes as we wished and carry on with the massage. I was immediately selected by a youngish man, so had no problem of choice. The rest of the group took about five minutes to settle with a partner. One girl kept on her panties, another her bra and panties – the rest of us were naked. We massaged one another in pairs, as instructed, for an hour, and then it was time for lunch.

Lunch was an opportunity for me to confirm that some of the group already knew one another and had much in common. Many of them were vegetarians and practised yoga. Most had previous experience of massage, some with the others in the group. Different from the emotional confrontation groups there was much talk about what had happened, about the techniques and benefits of massage, related topics and mysticism and philosophy.

Then back again for more massage. First with our previous partners and then to change if we wished. All but one couple, two men, changed partners. We continued for a two-hour session, and were agreed the time passed quickly.

A point of interest arose during that afternoon session. Most encounter group leaders lay great stress on honesty in personal relationships – in conversations particularly. (Many of them put a premium on apparently ruthless, even vicious, frankness.) We were asked to observe some different rules. Not to say, for example,

'That's too hard' or 'That hurts' but instead 'I like that very much, but it would be better softer,' or 'That feels very good, but it would feel better still if it were more gentle.' The rule seemed to work well. What other encounter leaders would have claimed was going on 'under the skin' I cannot imagine but I was encouraged to find at least one sector of the movement able to use the pleasing lubricants of courtesy and consideration in the interests of interpersonal communication.

After the two-hour session we went to a nearby restaurant. It was a tribute to the leader and the day's work that there was a reluctance to leave -- even for food. (The massage, although gentle and affectionate, had made us all hungry.)

We were keen to get back. We had established a group identity and wanted to get as much from it as we could. It had taken over two hours for the group to relax and unity to grow. But tensions and inhibitions had, in the main, gone and we were happy to be naked together. For example, there was no longer any effort made to disguise, or look away from, the erections and part erections that had previously been a source of unease. (In passing I might make it clear that the rest of the day had been taken up with full body massage, from the toes to the head. Every part of the body had been smoothed and stroked equally, with one exception : although there had been no embargo on touching pubic areas, in fact, without explicit manœuvring, these parts had been avoided.)

After more mutual massage it was time for questions and discussion. This was free and easy and related exclusively to matters of technique and did not touch personal relationships. It led us to discuss different kinds of massage and a new method was demonstrated by the leader -- the transmission of energy through approximated hands. In pairs we closed our eyes and held out our hands, palms horizontal, one facing up and the other down, palm above palm to partner. We moved them sometimes in unison and sometimes apart; sometimes in touch and sometimes from a distance. Many found it to be more intimate than the full body massage. It confirmed for them the validity of what encounter enthusiasts call non-verbal communication, although from time to time, like the conditioned verbalisers we were, some of us opened our eyes and talked about the experiences. Full marks to the leader for not preventing us.

This session brought us to the end. We were sad to leave and there was much procrastination, hugging and kissing. Two things stayed to tease my mind. First: in a body massage group, all the explicit relaxation exercises were verbally directed and undertaken individually. Second: the insistence on the release of psychic energy through those places normally kept private! I had given them little thought before – those areas *between* the fingers and toes. I found this intriguing and have lived with my fingers and toes in a new way ever since.

GOINGS-ON OR ON-GOING

I attended many other group meetings and spoke with group leaders in Canada, the United States and Great Britain. One of the most unlikely events took place in New York. It was organised in the evening and we were due to 'encounter' from seven thirty to ten thirty. As it happened, there was no encounter during the session, that is unless a three-hour lecture from the leader's 'major disciple practising in the States' can be called an encounter.

There were eighteen of us quietly waiting for the mysteries to begin when it was revealed I was from England and a newcomer to the group. I admitted the condition and was singled out for a 'few words to set it all up'. The few words became a three-hour lecture exclusively *at me*, or so it felt. The rest of the group sat politely until the end of the session and then left in silence. Much of the time had been spent in eulogising the master (who, over a period of six months, I had never been allowed to meet), the rest in mystical descriptions: 'journal-externalisation-climaxes' reached through 'body-meditation, camera-ladders and stepping-stone logs'.

It was all so obtuse, and mystically esoteric that it defied my rational understanding. The rest of the group seemed to understand and appreciate it being said again and again, or so the head nodding and noise-making suggested. Perhaps part of the explanation lies in the fact that the master is reputed to refuse 'to advise, to judge, to help, to sympathise or be aggressive – or even to be a catalytic agent or response-making organism made manifest'. This is acceptable (in spite of the jargon) but for the organisation's national advertising. It seemed ironic (if not dishonest) that money should be spent on publicity campaigns to bring people to the feet of a master who, self-confessedly, wished 'merely to be'.

Then there was the group that invited me to observe – once they had established I was not a practising psychiatrist. During my research it had been difficult to get invitations to spectate and I had understood. Here was a group that told me I would be able to participate only if I was in current practice as a medic, psychologist or psychiatrist. When I explained the general nature of my interest I was straightway invited to watch. I was told if I did this for a six-month period, twice a week, it would be possible to consider me for membership. Although they advertised their sessions as encounter meetings they spoke of them exclusively as group therapy and were adamant they were suited only to the expert. When I asked 'expert in what?' I got no answer. Being expert, experienced or trained came up often with this group and, although it was never stated, I gained the impression they meant professional training in psychiatry.

There were those groups who had moved from encounter to drug abuse prevention or gone into education. 'We've shut down the whole shop. Now we restrict our work to children – its much more rewarding.'

There were others too, 'We used to do dance therapy, reality therapy and everything in between, but now we just do finger painting' and 'The whole things off, actually, we're starting a commune in the spring.'

I met one leader who told me she had 'been on groups' for five years before she had ventured into leading one herself, 'but, you see, I was well prepared for it by five years with my analyst.' Many other leaders spoke of the support role of analysis, hypnotherapy, and massage. Just as many spoke of the destructive role of psychiatrists, hypnotherapists and masseurs in what was 'a personal thing – a people thing'.

There were those who were on drugs and those who were off; those for meditation and those for contemplation (the differences were explained to me at length at one meeting, but I am still unaware); there were those who felt 'kinetic-non-verbal-inter-personal-relationships' were essential and those who would not allow any body contact; there were those who were for 'talk, talk, talk – it all out', and those who permitted only abstract vocalisation. I came across a group that insisted on complete silence in all their sessions.

Most individuals in the groups had more in common than their sociocultural background – 'middle class/intellectual'. They all seemed frustrated by their personal and professional lives. In so far as the 'sick get well, the well get better' they belonged to the well and not the sick. But underpinning the whole movement was a sense of deep frustration. (I shall not forget the case of the middle-aged lady I met at three groups. She was charming and attractive to everyone. Her husband had sent her to encounter sessions. He found her too difficult to live with. He refused to attend.)

There was the architect who had been on three eight-day sessions, one marathon and was a member of two on-going groups. He felt the movement improved his life in a way he 'would not have believed possible'. His wife, friends and colleagues agreed he had changed, but for the worse. They said he had lost his sense of humour, his charm, compassion and understanding and had become so aggressively self-assertive it was difficult to recognise or like him. His wife eventually left him.

I saw a girl run away from a group in near hysteria. She bumped into a wall in her hurry, tripped and fell. She was in hospital for three weeks. When I interviewed her there she claimed she had been 'driven too far . . . to the point of collapse'.

There were couples who were loyal to one another in spite of taunting evidence supplied by the group and there were couples who took every opportunity to expose their marital grievances in public. The general judgment of encounter experts was that the latter type of relationship was 'more honest'.

I could cite many cases of individuals who said they gained nothing but a sense of personal purposelessness; of couples who claimed their marriages had been ruined; of girls who had been terrified and of men who had been driven by impotent fury into infantile tantrums. Some felt the movement encouraged outright rudeness and some felt the groups were hothouses of uncontrolled emotional exhibitionism.

To end this chapter on such a note would be to misrepresent the majority who felt they gained some release, personal awareness, purpose and growth. Although almost all reported a falling-off of benefits after a time, varying between days and months, the majority claimed the carry-over was worthwhile. I found no evidence to support this.

To end it without reference to my attempts to place advertising copy in the local and national press would be to omit a revealing area. The advertisement I tried to place seemed *to me* straightforward and harmless. It read as follows:

VOLUNTEERS INVITED FOR NEW ENCOUNTER GROUP TO BE FORMED
SINGLES AND COUPLES WELCOME
MARATHON AND ON-GOING GROUPS
NO FEES AT FIRST — JUST ENTHUSIASM

There was to be a box number.

I had great difficulty in placing the advertisement at all. The following comments from the advertising manager of a well-known weekly are representative of the many refusals I received. He was explaining why copy was carefully scrutinised and much rejected:

'Words like "couples", "body" and "massage" are not acceptable by us. Not that there is anything wrong in the words, but there are unfortunate connotations and rather "con" ads that come through at the moment and we just had to — because of the complications in this — we just had to make a strict rule on some words. Massage must not appear under any circumstances. It's like other things like hypnotherapy, probably a very good practice when practised by an expert, but you've got to be damned careful about these things and therefore the British Code of Advertising Practice says don't touch it. These are just protective devices so far as we are concerned so that people shan't be taken in, and consequently a lot of innocent advertisers suffer.'

Here is one of the replies I received when finally the copy was accepted :

Dear Sir,
   I am interested in joing [sic] your proposed organisation either in singles, doubles, in threes or groups as my ex-wife left for good for Poland as she was an ex-Polish refugee. There are no family tyes or divorce complications and I feel extremely lonely sometimes. Should your organisation is what I have in mind I will pay you well.
FROM : INTERESTED

   MR TED ALAN FLEETWOOD – Aged 38 years, 5ft 8in tall, hazel eyes, dark brown hair, medium size, likes sport, animals, pictures and is a very *keen* heterosexual + (PLUS)

A third of the letters were similar. A third actually knew what encounter groups were. The other third wrote because they had no idea what it was about and wanted further details.

In the beginning *I* had little idea what it was about and *I* wanted further details. After more than fifty group sessions, in Britain, Canada and the States, spread over more than a year, I responded mainly to the irony, the supreme irony of an encounter movement, searching, as it claims, after truth and honesty, yet seducing its devotees with masks and charms of intriguing fantasy. Relating becomes more important than the object of the relationship; the masks become the face and the means becomes an end.

Many leaders, however, were still in touch with the hard facts of reality – perhaps because they spelt money. Many of them had fears for the future. Fears that untrained personnel – 'self-seeking charlatans' is how one leader described them – would rise to leadership within the movement and destroy its purpose and validity. The circle turns yet again and fantasy confronts fantasy, mask encounters mask and even the leaders rationalise their responses when their positions (and incomes) are threatened.

But let me repeat : most customers are more than satisfied with the service they buy. They claim it to be better than any other and better than the advertisements state. Who knows? Perhaps they are right and the means is a better end than the end itself.

In Canada and the States most of my enquiries met a situation reflected by this typical tape-recorded message I heard in New York : 'If you're calling about the encounter group – the whole thing's off.' This may be the case in North America. In Britain the message would surely be : 'If you're calling about the encounter group – the whole thing's on.' On, have-on, come-on or on-going?

JUST GOOD FRIENDS
The Contact Organisations

There are many agencies purporting to exist exclusively to serve people who need people who need people. Many are highly organised; some are computerised and a few are one-man industries run from living-rooms.

What first caught my attention was the variety in advertising. It ranged from a few, almost concealed, words in a naturist magazine, inserted once only, to regular, expensive spreads in the national dailies and weeklies. I discovered some had a telephone answering service and others were without a phone. Some replied within twenty-four hours and others took more than a month. Fees varied considerably – from pennies and cents to dollars and pounds. They had two practices in common: they requested personal details from me; they used plain, sealed envelopes. The contents of the latter varied even more than the advertising.

I must have received every possible combination and permutation of paper, print and lay-out. One envelope contained roughly torn-off, once white, duplicating paper. There was no name, address, date or reference – just an unheaded application form and questionnaire. (I can still only guess at the organisation that might have sent it.) I received coarse-fibred missives in garish colours, one with vivid pink and yellow stripes, and also carefully presented expensive, glossies. The following example was one of the first to arrive.

It was a pink circular with my name inserted in biro. It contained blanks for my personal details. The agency claimed I was specially qualified for the privilege of a reduced fee. It read: 'Simply state overleaf your age, height, build, colour of hair/eyes, occupation. A brief description of characteristics, hobbies, interests, and particulars of desired partner.' Turning over, I expected to find at least some kind of spacing or ruling. There was nothing. I was expected to use the blank side of the duplicated circular. It was a poor recommendation to a service that described itself as 'personal, special and confidential'. It was written 'in all sincerity' and signed (duplicated) 'yours very sincerely'.

Another organisation expressed the following sentiments on a printed brochure:

'Something wonderful will come into your Lonely Life when you send to me and join this Worldwide Bureau.

The very next Day you will receive a membership number, and lists of other people who wish to banish their Empty, Pointless, Meaningless Existence. You cannot Live Life to the full unless it is shared. All you have to do is to sit at home over a Cup of Tea and select all the people you want to know — its as easy as that — No Fuss — No Bother....

People of all classes and types, come to me with Sadness in their Hearts, but never leave without a Sparkle in their eyes, and New Hope for their Future. "I feel better already, after talking to you," is often said to me.

What a lovely job I have making others happy.

I am truly Grateful for the Opportunity. Let me Help You. Sincerely and with every Good Wish.

THE DIRECTOR'

An agency that presented itself on glossy yellow, red and white sheets gave pages of self praise to introduce a remarkably brief application form. All they wanted was: name and address, age and sex. Many sent out-of-date lists, brochures and magazines. Some of them carried only a typed addendum, 'write for further details'. More than one represented itself as a correspondence club, but I soon discovered the phrase 'wishes to write to' was a euphemism for a more intimate relationship.

Some organisations used different names in different advertisements and some altered key words when describing themselves. Since they used box numbers it was not until similar circulars proved to be from one address that the masquerade was uncovered.

I wrote to supposedly different clubs catering for naturists, astrologists, orientals, homosexuals – each advertising a unique exclusive service. They transpired to be one and the same with one list of contacts.

At least half the agencies wrote a second time, offering a reduction of fee if I replied within a week. A few offered a third reduction. Some sent vouchers and some sent special letters. Some sent a copy of the original circular with the fee changed and a PS written in. One foolscap sheet, covered with close print, had this *duplicated* at the bottom: 'This is a note specially for *you*. I feel *certain* I can help *you* to find *true* happiness!'

Many of the organisations claimed the backing of clergy, medical practitioners, psychiatrists, psychologists and 'personality consultants'. All of them claimed their services were discreet and confidential – one claiming that 'not even the staff' saw the correspondence. In spite of these claims, my different personae received letters from unapproached organisations. Many people I spoke to relied on the confidence being absolute. Some men were really worried as they were using the organisations unbeknown to their wives.

FORM AND FORMS

Some of the questionnaires were comprehensive and some were plain nosey. The following example *does not exist except in these pages*. It is merely typical of those I received:

NAME   ADDRESS   TELEPHONE (optional)
AGE   SEX   OCCUPATION   RELIGION (optional)
Height   Weight   Clouring   Skin   Hair   Eyes
I am: Serious – Confident – Extrovert – Lighthearted – Shy – Gay – Mix easily – Good talker – Good listener. Married – Separated – Divorced – Single
I have...... children   I like/do not like children
Smoker – cigarettes or pipe   Drinker – Regular or Social
House owner   Car owner   Do you drive?
What are your politics?   Is your hair long?

Answer 'yes' or 'no' to the following :

    Do you believe in marriage as a permanent institution?
    Do you want to see capital punishment reinstated?
    Do you prefer being indoors to out of doors?
    Are zoos a good thing?
    Is there a future for democracy?
    Do you have a strong sexual appetite?
    Do you have a favourite colour?
    Do you like art?
    Do you like sport?
    Do you think television should be censored?
    Are you in favour of extra-marital intercourse?
    Would you say you are tolerant?
    Do others say you are tolerant?
    Do you like cats?

List your interests: (Most agencies left this blank but one offered 144 possible choices.)

Some agencies probed my religion and politics, some ignored them. Some asked for details of personal income and property, some left it a voluntary area. One asked for the name and address of my bankers. Some of the forms referred to 'ethnic origin'. Here is the way one organisation approached it :

COLOURING :   Blonde or fair hair – pale skin
                Black or brown hair – pale skin
                Red, auburn or sandy hair – pale skin
                Colouring typical of Middle East
                Chinese, Japanese or other Oriental types
                Indian or Pakistani type colouring
                African or American Negro types.

I was asked to describe myself and indicate those I would not be prepared to meet.

Generally I used a 'neutral' persona as a model for the forms. It made me an average-type male who wanted to meet an average-type female. Occasionally I tried a test case and, required my choice to possess features not extreme or improbable, but specific and easily validated. For example : 'no taller than five feet', or 'fair haired' or 'Oriental'. With these requests I placed an embargo on any other type. The agencies did not guarantee to meet my requirements, but they did guarantee *not to introduce me to anyone without them*. In the flesh my dates bore no relation to my selection or rejection of characteristics. There was a one-to-one relationship between the average type requirements and the specials.

The influential factors appeared to be age and access. All my dates were in the same age bracket and most of them lived within twenty-five miles. They had found only the same two criteria to be identifiable. Two women in particular were angry about meeting short men when they had specified no man under six feet. The women were both six feet and disliked being accompanied by men shorter than themselves. They said they had remonstrated without effect.

The physical, psychological, emotional and sexual make-up of my partners, in spite of specific questionnaires, seemed random factors. For example, one date should have had a 'large sexual appetite'. Within five minutes she told me that she would never 'get into bed with a man without a ring' and 'sexual contact was unpleasant because of its unhygienic nature' – later spelling out mouth to mouth kissing and sexual intercourse. I could have been sympathetic had I made precipitate overtures but she offered her views gratuitously.

There was another. She wrote as a result of an application stating my interest as 'Platonic and non-erotic'. In her first letter she asked me to tell her of my emotional and sexual needs. Before I had had time to reply I received a long letter in which she wrote of some of her fantasies, all of which involved a 'large male organ' and 'rape'. How these mix-ups could occur with all the personal attention and computer guarantees is a mystery unless the 'personal service' is less important than the fee.

However, it is true that most of my dates and I could have got on (or even got off) if we had wished *to work at it*, but very few of them made any effort to read me or relate to me, preferring a passive role, sheltered from the dangers of making a false move and thus removed from any fear of failure.

At the time, these meetings seemed small return for the time and money spent. After longer in the twilight world of the alienated, I changed my mind, noting how many need the agencies as whipping boys to enable them to avoid the ultimate responsibility for their personal relationships. The business and its rituals provide a contraceptive skin protecting them from the dangers of real contact and creating 'false' situations in which they can hold back or switch off – ready to blame the system if the date does not work. Ironies littered the person-to-person scene, but this seemed the most ironic – that an agency explicitly set up to enable people to meet people, should itself become a major factor in helping them avoid meeting.

The word friendship appeared frequently in circulars and most people I interviewed or dated said that was what they were looking for. It was difficult to see how they hoped to achieve it without moving towards it. The meetings were often amiable enough but there was always hesitancy and even fear of contact. Some dates were understandably suspicious of the men they met – they claimed to have been treated to abrupt physical overtures – but most seemed to expect a no man's land of mere adjacency; content to be present without relating. More than a few explicitly said they would like such a partnership. It was almost as if there were commandments: 'Thou shalt see, hear and be present: Thou shalt not do nor be.' The last was sad: the denial of *being* and the acceptane of a flaccid role of non-self. I could see no hope of progress from amiability to friendship while the safety net of the system and the contraceptive role of non-self were so essentially present.

I asked a few dates outright what they were looking for. They all answered in abstractions so vague as to be meaningless. I gained the impression of them wishing not to say the wrong thing and so lose a possible partner. After a time I became more explicit and asked if they were looking for:

(a) friendship
(b) a non-erotic relationship

(c) an erotic relationship
(d) marriage

Those who came into (b) and (d) were extremely hesitant to say and those in (a) hardly less so. Only those in (c) were prepared to make an immediate and definite commitment.

Some agencies sent me dates one at a time and I would ask for the next; others sent block of four to six at a time and others sent lists of names and addresses covering the whole country. To some I wrote and some I telephoned – some contacted me.

Here are a few of my 'intimate personal confrontations'. . . .

Mary and Gwenda from Dover
Although the two cases were separated by more than a month and to the best of my knowledge the two ladies did not know each other, they came from the same town and from the same agency. They were the only two dates the agency sent.

Over a period of two months I tried to ring Mary and on each occasion was told she was 'at work', 'on holiday', 'ill' or just plain 'away'. I believe I spoke to Mary – it was always the same voice – and for her own reasons she had no wish to meet or know about me. What made it intriguing was precisely the same sequence with Gwenda. Always the same voice, the same reported absence, the offer to let her know I had rung. In the end, the same result, no contact.

I report this case first, because one of the hazards in the game is the high failure rate : people already suited; people who had lost interest; people who never had been interested but got involved and wished they hadn't. There were those, like Mary and Gwenda, who were permanently absent.

I complained to the agency about Mary. There were fulsome apologies and promises to do better next time. They sent me Gwenda's details.

Mollie Butters
Here I made contact, but not without difficulty. First by telephone :

D.B. I'm from the XYZ agency.

M.B. Actually you've chosen a very bad moment. I've got a boy-friend here and – a married one – this is partly why I wrote to XYZ. I seem to be surrounded by married men – I've been married and I'm in the throes of being divorced and – it is very inconvenient – could you ring me back later on? I think he's leaving fairly soon. He's been very good to me – but he's also. . . . Say before half past – no quarter past eight – when I'm off to 'Keep Fit'.

LATER

M.B. Well, I'll tell you . . . from my side I've been disappointed. Yes. I've met some very nice people and its been very enjoyable, but the only one I've wanted to see again was the typical-bachelor-have-a-good-time-type and although I liked this I wanted someone a bit more sincere – and wasn't willing to give up what I'd got just for another casual affair. . . .

D.B. Tell me about yourself.

M.B. It'll have to be brief because this friend's arrived. Sounds awfully vain this but . . . fairly attractive and rather on the plump than the skinny side for my height – I'm only five feet two – just under five feet two – but it doesn't seem to have mattered in my life. I've been married fourteen years. I got married very young and it was a disaster. But have a lovely child and don't regret that a bit.

As I was saying briefly before, I've never met anyone in a similar position to me or a single man and I get a bit fed up with all the married men around here that want to take me out because their wives don't understand them and it's only going to end up in heartbreak for someone. I get a bit lonely – I'm very fond of company and I just don't like being on my own too much.

We arranged to meet later in the week in a hotel foyer of Mollie's choice at nine in the evening. I arrived early. At 9.30, with no sign of her and no message, I rang. She said she was sorry not to be there but her baby-sitter had failed to arrive and she just hoped I would ring. She gave me complicated directions to get to her house. When I finally arrived she apologised again — this time for misdirecting me — she had thought I was coming from another place.

The apologies continued. She was sorry she had not told me she had four children. 'You might not have wanted to bother.' In fact she had just taken in two more children who had been deserted by their mother. The house seemed too small for six children and five cats.

I was received warmly and found that Mollie had described herself accurately — fairly attractive and plump. She made coffee (having told me on the phone she had nothing to drink, but if I wanted to bring some I was to feel free). Mollie Butters had met five men through the agency, with only one of whom she was not angry. He had been the pleasant bachelor who wanted nothing more than a jolly social time, mainly drinking. Two had tried to 'rape' her and the remaining two had proposed marriage within thirty minutes of meeting. One man had treated Mollie to tales of his previous date. (I discovered the man and I had dated the same lady in the same week. I had been treated to his description by the lady in question — Brenda Moore.) Mollie found it greatly amusing.

Not amusing, however, was the situation in which I found myself. At ten thirty Mollie asked if I would co-operate with her. I agreed and discovered she wanted me to be 'the man who was looking at the room' — her reason being the apparently imminent arrival of a local taxi driver. (He was the married man mentioned on the phone and it was his habit to call after dropping his last fare.) Mollie said how 'good' he was for her — in finance, sex and free transport — and she did not want to upset him. With her request for a 'little white lie', out came the whole story.

The taxi driver would not leave his wife. In spite of what Mollie had said earlier she was *not* in the throes of divorce and did not expect to be. She wanted a partner more permanent than the taxi driver since she was confident his wife would discover the affair and end it. Until she found someone more promising she did not propose to disturb her entente, 'but it would be all right if I said I had come about the room because he knows I'm looking for another lodger'. I was warned he would expect to stay and I would have to go. I found the situation complicated and wondered how she expected to establish that anyone else would be a satisfactory permanent partner while the taxi driver continued his nightly visits.

Not only had Mollie Butters taken in the two children who had been deserted by their mother – she had taken in father as well. And, moreover, there was a philosophy lecturer also living there. They were both, in her own words, 'good to her'. (With children, cats and men who were good to her, it was Milk Wood out of H. E. Bates.)

Since Mollie had described the taxi driver as an ogre more than once I decided discretion was the better part of curiosity and left her to the care of her experts.

Explanation of Mollie's case seems to lie in what she told me of her marriage. Her husband had been an active homosexual and, although they had produced four children, she had never experienced orgasm until a year after he left her. She seemed to be adequately compensating for wasted time and lost opportunities.

Brenda Moore

The case was arranged through an agency that claimed that we were one of the best matched couples they had ever achieved! Brenda was a tall – six feet and a half inch tall – unattractive woman in her late forties. She was a State Registered Nurse. It so happens I cannot stand the sight of blood. We had little in common.

For someone searching for a life-partner she had much to learn. She took the lead as if I were an incapable and stupid geriatric, never once actually listening to a word I said. In fact she listened to no one, seeming unaware of the rest of the world.

She felt strongly about brown-eyed men – claiming them to be unbalanced, moody, neurotic, unstable, introverted and inhibited (that is unless extrovert and arrogant!) Also: 90 per cent of asthmatics had brown eyes and so had alcoholics. (My eyes are brown and Brenda wore spectacles with thick lenses.)

She told me, with pride, how successfully she had treated her mother, father and sister, who were all neurotics. Her sister had had a 'disastrous first marriage and is much better with her second husband, although he is an alcoholic'. The saga continued. Her father was an alcoholic – and so were many neuro-surgeons with whom she worked. (All this while consuming port-and-lemon, and gin-and-tonic.) This led to hair-raising stories of battered babies.

Brenda introduced me to the hotelier's widow – she had treated the husband in the last stages of sclerosis – brought on by alcoholism. I was told intimate details of his symptoms and background. The evening continued. . . .

As we parted Brenda asked if she had been what I had expected. Before I had a chance to reply she told me I was exactly what she had expected, and insisted she meant it as a compliment. This made me a much better person for all of two days.

Rosemary House

Mrs House was the one date I had from an agency which ignored me for more than six weeks after I had paid the fees and returned the forms. In the end they somewhat reluctantly agreed to let me have my four promised contacts. I received one. I rang her. . . .

R.H. I was married into the Foreign Service, having worked in it and was a very happy wife for seventeen years. My husband is now in Kenya having married again and I work for a professor of pure mathematics. I don't know anything about your world—journalism, that is. I hate journalese and journalists but I read a lot—which I love next to politics. Are you pink, blue or red or what?

D.B. A bit red, I suppose.

R.H. Oh, I see. [falling inflections] I'm strong right-wing in practically everything. Orthodox and conservative in capital letters and italics. [A long pause.] Let me see—what did the Foreign Service teach one? How to put on . . . how to act a bit I suppose. What else did they teach you? Canasta . . . and dreadful things like that . . . and they teach one cooking and all that. . . but I like being out of doors and I do like beagling. It's mostly standing about watching hounds being completely stupid but I do like to feel the wind in my *hair* after London. I love *hare* don't you? I love roast—not very good at jugged. The only thing is the meat's so dark it's bound to put people off a bit. You should look around now and go to your fishmonger—but you'll only be able to eat a tiny bit of it. The ones the hounds don't get are generally shot. . . .

There was more but eventually we agreed to meet for a drink at her flat the following week.

I dressed not to offend her conservative orthodoxy and found her suite in an expensive block of flats in Kensington. The following note was stuck to the letter box:

VERY SORRY BUT I CAN'T REMEMBER YOUR NAME. HAVE HAD A SURPRISE OPPORTUNITY TO GO OUT TO DINNER AND THE THEATRE FOR MY BIRTHDAY AND I CAN'T SAY NO.

There were other memorable cases. The lady who told me within two minutes of being on the phone that her seven children had 'nits in their heads'. She bred polecats and lived with a pop group that kept a snake in their bedroom.

There was an Australian lady who ran a guest house, a charring business and a plastic thatching service. There was a German girl who sold wigs for men, magnetic door numbers and name plates. (She told me not to arrive in a car because males were a menace on the roads and should not be allowed, especially driving lorries, 'They're just not safe. Mad; all of them, raving mad.')

Although the area of the contact organisations was prone to a failure rate of many kinds, I actually met people through most of the agencies I used. The majority of my dates felt they were getting value for money. Some felt they were getting nothing, but they expected nothing and were not distressed. There were only a few who thought they had cause to complain. This was not the case in the next field I covered.

CORRESPONDENCY?

Pen clubs

Almost all operate in a similar way: payment of the membership fee brings a list of names and addresses of people wishing to write to other people, complete with guarantees that the people selected are *genuine* with their interests sifted and sorted to preclude incompatibility. I received many of these lists and a high proportion were out of date. Most of them used a key to denote members' details: age, sex, interests, etc. I was promised with unfailing regularity that, after paying my entrance fee, I was sure to receive letters straight away and this was supported by quotes from those who were 'completely satisfied' with the clubs' services.

It was a cheat and a fraud. I wrote more than a hundred letters and spent over £20 to have my name circulated to people who in theory were anxious to write to me. To this day I have received not a single reply (I accept of course the possibility that I write off-putting letters) nor have I had the benefit of the promised 'pleasant surprise' through the post. I don't object to the way the system treated me, since I am not an inveterate letter writer. In my mind is the image of those who needed and waited for replies, since there seem to be many people wanting to write to somebody. Such a failure rate can only exacerbate a lonely, inadequate situation. It is probably better to do nothing, than to attempt an improvement and later feel, not only as lonely as ever, but also rejected.

The joys of literary companionship offered would satisfy a mind far more imaginative than mine. I was to be approached, through the post, by personalities, all of whom were attractive, charming, friendly, cultured, intelligent, well-educated, good looking and not one of them old or elderly. In fact, from over five hundred, only one was even middle aged. (I was able to check some bona fides and found at forty-two, by their standards, I was not only young but in nonage.) In addition to this general charisma were the many exotic characters: female vampirists, homosexual taxi drivers, transvestite window dressers, fourteen-year-old 'virgins', lesbian canine enthusiasts and bi-sexual witches. They may all have been pseudo. I heard from none.

One correspondence club used three different business names and addresses for different advertisements. I traced all three to an accommodation address run by an entirely different contact organisation. The address was also used by two contact magazines.

Non-events

A similar result came from many of the clubs that were supposed to put me in touch with people who organised social events in my locality. The following is typical:

I received a duplicated list of the people in my area who, I was led to believe, were busy arranging social events for me and others like me. The long list of telephone numbers suggested I might spend at least a month attending activities.

The first on the list lived with her sister. Correction – used to live with her sister. By the time I phoned she had left. Her sister told me she had never been to a function and had never heard of one actually happening. The second agreed she *was* a member, but didn't quite know what it was, since she had never been to a function. She did know another girl on the list and thought she had been to something once – believed this other girl had been skating – but she wasn't sure.

The pattern went on: two had married and no longer belonged, but they had never been anywhere or done anything. Four had left the area and couldn't be traced. One man was to be contacted through a friend's telephone, but was never there.

The longest telephone call was made by my wife:

M.W. Well there's a snag in actual fact – there's absolutely nothing doing. Nothing at all. There never has been; not from the very beginning. You know there just doesn't seem to be anybody doing anything at all. I think in actual fact the thing has died a hideous death. I was talked into it for water-skiing and skin-diving — but nobody does anything. I've had sort of vague people sort of phone me up over the last two years and say 'Whats' doing?' and I say 'Quite frankly absolutely nothing', and they say 'Oh dear how sad we thought this might be the case', 'What a shame.' You sound young. Are you?

J.B. No.

M.W. You sound terribly young. You don't even sound in the age group to . . . [laughs]. You've just joined have you? [Pause] You wouldn't like to [pause] well, my dear, actually I wondered if you'd like to . . . but I suppose you'd be sort of too young.

J.B. What had you in mind?

M.W. Well, nothing my dear, really — I suppose you'd be too young. [Laughs] By now.

The enigma teased us for some time.

Marriage markets

I had not intended to get involved with the marriage brokers. I saw them as distinct and beyond my research. I was contacted by them as a result of answering advertisements for friendly contacts. (I suppose it was my cynicism that had ruled marriage out of such dealings.)

On the friendship side of the marriage business the most interesting aspect was the number of ladies who wanted to write rather than meet. I conducted lengthy correspondence with five ladies (much more successful than the pen clubs) but when it came to meeting there was real reluctance — just another irony. In its way it was quite pleasing — the letters were affectionately busy and under different circumstances I can imagine being pleased to receive them. As it was, they seemed an excuse for not meeting, as if encounters were better described than executed, and although many letters told of what might happen if we were to meet, their style virtually denied the possibility.

I received lists which also seemed destined to prevent meetings, rather than encourage them. Here are a few selected items:

UNDER 55
REF. 276DT – BRISTOL 5ft 2in
(TEACHER) Divorced. Home loving, theatre and walks,
entertaining, has lived abroad. Seeks prof. or business
gent NOT a teacher, practical.

Ref. LN0071. Mary is 38, but looks younger. She is tall with
lovely long black hair hanging over her shoulders, dark com-
plexioned, black eyes, her own teeth and 34in bust, 26in waist
and 38in hips. Mary comes from a good family. She doesn't drink,
smoke or gamble. She had a boy-friend for a long time but
always kept pure. One evening she was drugged by him and he
had intercourse with her without her knowledge. It was a shock
to her and she saw him no more. This only sad act had made
her pregnant.

Mary speaks beautifully, likes music and moths and would be a
wonderful partner to a suitable gentleman who loves children.
She would like to be suited fairly soon. Why not give her a
chance if you would too?

Ref. LNS0321 I am Betsy Jane. I own a house and was born
in 1910 and am 5ft 4in. My bust is very firm, I have a well
defined figure, 44in–32in–40in. I weigh now 12st with no family.
I can give the man of my choice very good LOVE in every sense
of the word, given time. I want to be wanted, to be loved, and
to give L.O.V.E. Sex to me is essential and to be honest I fancy
a widower who also needs a good sex life, with a clean woman.

ADULTS ONLY!

The Contact Magazines

SOFT COVER OR HARD SELL?

I came by contact magazines in a number of ways. Some appeared in my letter box, presumably as a result of cross fertilisation or the kind offices of a cheeky friend. Some were pushed furtively into my hand in the back-streets of London and Toronto. Some were bought under the counter and some over it; some were offered by street vendors and some, although well advertised, required a subscription.

I approached them with an attitude of mind neither sentimentally naïve nor cynically jaded. I tried to retain the persona of a newcomer who took the descriptions at face value. Very few of the magazines mentioned 'sexual contacts' or 'sexual relationships'. Some of them described themselves as follows: Make Adult Contacts – Personal Advertisements – Genuine Friendship Seekers – Make Penfriends – Make Adult Friends – Get to Know Others – Don't be Lonely – Get Together – Get to Know Males, Females and Couples – Today's Most Exciting Newspaper.

The small magazines were often sold with their covers sealed by sticky tape. The larger newspaper editions were open for inspection. The contents were similar: stories of a sexual nature, advertisements for erotic books and objects, personal advertisements. The proportion varied from publication to publication and from issue to issue but central to all were the advertisements.

Some contained jokes and line sketch cartoons. The cartoons were not the only visuals. There were line drawings of the sexual aids advertised, and sometimes photographs, as remarkable for their bad reproduction as for pubic detail. Most photographs were intended to be erotic and some might even have had talent near them at one time. Economy won, aesthetics lost and the results were, by all standards, poor.

A special feature with some publications was photographs of the advertisers. Some were of couples, some were of single males, but the majority were of single females. They were mainly unclothed with faces blanked out and/or 'vital' parts covered or obscured by the pose. It was unusual to find a revealing nude with an identifiable face.

BOASTING, CONFESSING OR ASKING FOR ADVICE?

The advertisements were almost always couched in ambiguous terms and some were deliberately misleading. It was only after careful study that the meanings became clear. The tyro has to face difficult semantics. This is not a personal judgment only — many couples I met, experienced swingers, were unaware of the significance of some advertisements. (A number of men my wife met claimed they had been misled for a long time, believing all the advertisements to be from ladies sincerely seeking companionship.)

Just a few examples of the language and abbreviations will demonstrate the point: Strict Educationist — AC/DC — TV enthusiast — French Speaking — English Expert — Greek Speaking — Arabian Artist — Latin Lover — Roman Specialist — 'O' and 'A' levels needed — B & B — BO Treated — Rubber, Leather, Wood or Metal work instruction — DIY Fan.

The list is by no means complete and it is not intended as a quick guide for the novice. Hidden in the above are invitations to cunnilingus, fellatio, anal intercourse, bondage, spanking, whipping and other forms of restraint; masturbation; transvestite games as well as other services for hetero, homo and bi-sexuals.

Some of the advertisements were misleading and meant to be so. Others were frank:

Our daughter is very lonely. She is a college girl and has little time for courting. We would like to introduce her to a gentle, repeat gentle, man.

I would like to meet a pleasing young man. I am a hard-working girl and have little time for socialising. I don't like not knowing boys.

Artist's widow in her late fifties would like to meet genteel man for friendship. Must be cultured.

The euphemisms (as opposed to the downright misleading) come thick and fast. Generally there are references to 'business-men' or 'kind', 'kindly', 'generous' or 'spenders' to indicate there will be some kind of financial transaction. When this is otherwise the statement is brief and clear—NO FEES. (But this is not entirely to be trusted.)

After the middle range of the spectrum, which takes up most of the space, come the more frank statements :

'Tall, tanned redhead, 5ft 9in, 39in–26in–40in, really loves sex – can't get enough. Let me have it soon. Pay first.'

'Attractive male offers free board in exchange for sex.'

'We are two Lesbian girls who like showing what we do for sex. Like to come and watch us – it'll cost you though !'

I was contacted by no one who actually wanted a *lasting friendly relationship* – with or without sex. The nearest were replies from three different advertisers. Each returned a short note thanking me for my enquiry and letting me know they were suited. (They may well have been just putting me off but I like to think those three at least were genuine.) Apart from these, my hundreds of letters – all with the famous SAE – brought no non-commercial reply. All were seeking instant sex with even more instant cash.

DISTAFF SIDE

My wife's advertisement ('Housewife, late thirties, ex-dancer, would like to meet men friends. Please write fully and frankly.') brought courteous replies – many of them offering, if not friend-ship at least a spirit of companionship. Most of the men seemed unable to form sexual relationships easily and were willing to pay

—in time, hospitality, entertainment as well as cash—for any kind gesture they received. Most of them sent a photograph and a well mannered letter of introduction. Indeed, many of the letters were intelligent, interesting and perfectly acceptable overtures.

Some of the approaches were frank but not offensive, referring, as they did, to 'a sexual relationship' or 'a friendship of growing physical intimacy'. Most of the letters contained a brief character description; some contained life histories; and a high proportion were from addresses validated in telephone and town directories.

This is an example :

> Dear Very Attractive Lady,
> Having read your invitation I should very much like to be allowed the very great privilege of hearing from you. I am just forty-five, happy-go-lucky and have a very kind nature which is inclined to make me an ideal play-toy for a lady who likes to relax and enjoy herself as I would always put your happiness and pleasure before my own. In my professional life I hold a position of trust with one of the airlines and I would always use absolute discretion. Every word which I have written in this letter is one hundred per cent genuine and very sincere and I sincerely hope that I am allowed the very great privilege of hearing from you and making your acquaintance.
> > Yours truly,
> > EDWARD C. SWANN

After a number of telephone calls and meetings it became clear there was little deception from the men. They looked like their photographs (many of the women's photographs had obviously been taken years earlier); their character descriptions were as accurate as they had any right to be; their motives seemed to be exactly what they had suggested and there was no undue pressure or indiscretion from any of them. Mostly they presented a genuine picture of loneliness with some attempt to do something about it. Many spoke touchingly of their gratitude and appreciation – for a few minutes telephone conversation, a letter, or a brief meeting. *Many were quite convinced they would find an attractive, permanent partner through the contact magazines.*

CASES

I received different responses. Usually the replies came scribbled on the back of my original letters. They were brief : 'Ring me' – or just a first name and a telephone number. Some were explicit, often quite different from the suggestion in the advertisement, 'Intercourse – 35 dollars an hour.' Brief as these were, there was no coyness or attempt to mislead. They were straightforward.

The failure rate was high. Over 50 per cent of my letters are still unanswered in spite of the SAE. This is partly explained by the many false advertisements – fifteen box numbers in one issue led back to a single advertiser. A further explanation is found in the vicarious enjoyment and fantasy sought by many subscribers. (I interviewed two men who advertised as young women.) I also met many subscribers who did nothing more than read their copies – almost every-one of which contained complaints and injunctions regarding replying (or more frequently *not* replying) to letters.

Only in one case, that of Joan Hagen, did I follow up connections where sexual and financial implications were made clear in my first dealings with the advertisers. It was those who set out to deceive with promises of friendship or companionship without strings with whom I stayed until the final disclosure of real intent. Many of the lonely men I met would make easy victims for a cash killing – no matter whether from fear of exposure (twice I faced threats to 'phone my wife), inadequacy or plain shyness.

In one of my plays, *Action*, there is a line 'We've been everywhere; seen everything; done the lot. Yeah – done the lot.' The claim was not to apply to me. I found I had no jaded palate. The experiences were often novel for me. Here are some. . . .

Anna

The advertisement read 'Lonely, but lovely, young lady would like to meet educated gentlemen for friendship and happy times.' I wrote a neutral note suggesting we might meet and see if we got on. Anna didn't even turn over my letter to reply. She scribbled in the margin. She gave details of her name, age, address and telephone number, inviting me to ring her so we could arrange to meet. She also enclosed a photograph, taken from the current edition of a glamour magazine.

I rang her and we had a pleasant chat, arranging to meet in a few days time. There was no mention of money, presents, fees or expenses. Anna claimed to be a lovely but lonely young girl. She supported this by describing her work as a model and complaining that the only men she met wanted to take her photograph or to take her!

The address turned out to be a small block of council flats. I had been given rather complicated instructions about the colours of the doors I was to look for and, feeling a little anxious, I tapped on the door I thought was Anna's. It was red and had been left ajar. An arm sneaked through the opening and I was drawn into the hallway. The next events took place simultaneously and more quickly than I can describe them. Anna said, 'I like men with brown eyes – what colour are yours? Ooh! Don't you look like Omar Sharif?' She had one hand on my arm and another on my neck. Walking backwards she led me into a room and literally threw me on to the bed. Fortunately her aim was good. There was no other furniture in the room. I was later to discover it was the only furniture in the flat.

By this time Anna, dressed in brief bra, pants and negligée, was lying on top of me, kissing me and saying, 'Would you like a cup of coffee now; or later. Ooh! Let's have it later.' The proceedings went no further. There was an interruption. An old lady walked in, Anna must have left the outer door ajar, and spoke abruptly. She wanted there to be no noise! Anna replied even more abruptly 'Get stuffed'. With a nice sense of timing her visitor said: 'No dear; I leave that to you' and walked out.

Anna seemed to find the incident hilarious. She said the old lady's bark was worse than her bite and that she often complained of the banging (huge joke this) but was the only tenant who knew what was happening, the rest believing her to be a book-keeper whose clients visited her because she was physically handi-capped. She made various jokes about the real nature of her physical handicap and also debit, credit, entries and withdrawals.

It was informally established that Anna was a business girl who charged £5. There was no apology for the deception but Anna's gay vitality made it difficult to be angry or impatient with her, especially since she had made coffee and told entertaining stories. She told me of the hunchback who asked her if he could 'come twice for £20' (nice ambiguity) and explained that most girls would not 'receive him a second time'. Anna had agreed and had 'given the hunchback a very good time—although I say it myself'. After his second visit he had left her his double fee in an envelope. She didn't open it until he had left. It was stuffed with blank sheets of paper cut to the size of pound notes. Anna harboured no malice, just the memory of a cheeky incident that had amused her.

She told me of other men who had swindled her. Her attitude was always the same—if they had had the nerve and the wit to manage it 'Good luck to them'. During the hour I spent with her, Anna kept referring to her pleasure in her work. (I suppose the encounter jargon is 'job fulfilment'.) She claimed she got more out of it than most of her clients, more than once suggest-ing she ought to pay them. For Anna, sex was the greatest hobby going. She was a happy, randy kid who was good company. It was with goodwill I handed over the fee. We shook hands at the door.

Angela Osgood
The advertisement was yet another describing an attractive but lonely young lady who wished to meet a considerate gentleman. Her letter read as follows:

> Dear Mr B.,
> Many thanks for your letter. I wonder if you would

give me a telephone call at the above number, for a chat, as I do not like to write *to* [sic] many details in a letter. Hoping to hear from you again,

Yours sincerely,

ANGELA OSGOOD

(I found the spelling error interesting since later Angela claimed – as many advertisers did – to be a trained school-teacher. The details she gave me of her college, its courses and staff – all of which I happened to know well – suggested that she had at least been there.)

I rang as she requested and found myself talking to a giggly, pretentious female. Trying to impress, she used the right words in the wrong context, and drove her accent through remarkable vowel changes. I was instructed seven times how to get to the house – or rather, to a telephone kiosk near it. Particular emphasis was laid on elaborate ritual. I was to go to the kiosk, ring her and, when she answered, stand outside the kiosk so she could see me. She would then tell me if I was of suitable appearance. The neighbourhood was 'select, with a nice tone' and she did not want it lowered.

At the appointed hour I performed the ritual and was declared suitable. The special arrangements did not end there. Angela's mother-in-law was in the house, waiting to take her grandson out for the afternoon. I was told to introduce myself as the 'man from the insurance', come to see about the garage which had fallen down the week before. (From time to time during my research I was asked to be the man who had come about the room; the man who had come about the telephone; the man about the insurance, the washing-machine and the holiday in the Bahamas. I was also asked to be a 'friend of Ron's'; a 'friend of Daddy's'; a 'friend of Maggie's' and on one occasion a Samaritan!)

I was duly introduced to the mother-in-law and made polite noises in reply to her snobbish and gratuitous trivia. After a time she left and Angela and I settled down.

On the telephone she had enthused about her social position

and her son Jan. She returned to these topics now. I learned how he had to be introduced to officers in the Air Force and the Horse Guards at an early age to get used to mixing with them and thus guarantee a proper place in life. There were repeated references to his lessons in riding, swimming and dancing. Angela also confessed to thoughts of incest 'God knows what I'll do when he's fifteen or sixteen.' I also learned of this five-year-old paragon's tastes in food. He was unable to eat eggs, fish, milk or cheese and disliked meat since he thought it all to be chicken and had once had a pet hen. He also had a hernia.

In addition to these intimacies I was told that, while we were chatting, Angela's aged father-in-law was in the rear garden chopping down a pear tree. It was to help him overcome a heart attack.

The tone of the conversation was out of keeping with the repair and decoration of the house. The story of the garage falling down had been true and the house itself was in a pretty tumble-down state. Paint was peeling inside and outside. There was hardly a carpet and little furniture. The few chairs and tables were battered and dirty. The situation was incongruous.

After a description of 'grampa's' attack, Angela suddenly asked if I thought she was 'acceptable'. Without waiting for a reply she took me by the hand and rushed me upstairs into Jan's bed-cum-play room. She was undressed and on the bed in a matter of seconds, 'Oh! That's better.' I was completely clothed and a little unsure of my role in a set of circumstances that seemed straight from Eugene O'Neill.

The need for a decision was taken out of my hands since she spoke again, this time in a clipped voice: 'I didn't tell you before — I don't like being kissed. You'll have to use a rubber and I want £7 first.' It was easy to disclaim further interest, leave her fee and escape without loss of face on either side.

Lilly Pettit

Lily advertised as 'sympathetic to the moods of gentlemen — offering companionship and understanding'. Her reply to my letter asked me to ring her. We had a pleasant chat. Lily said it would be a good idea to meet and 'see how we get on – whether we're likely to strike a friendship'. I agreed and the date was made.

I went round in the early evening. It was a large boarding-house run, as I later discovered, by Lily. The ground floor was a maze of dark passages. Eventually Lily appeared and told me to follow her. We went through a further maze of passages. Lights were switched on and off. I was shown into a large bed-sitting room. There was a strange looking dog, messing on a sheet of hardboard. I was welcomed by shrieks : 'Give 'er a kiss! Give 'er a kiss.' Two mina birds had obviously been well trained! I was shown the other occupants of the room : twenty-five varieties of fish in twelve tanks and thirty-two birds in separate cages. After the conducted tour Lily turned to me and said, 'It doesn't smell birdy, does it?' In all fairness it didn't – there was just the unpleasant odour arising from the droppings of the dog. They received neither comment nor attention.

The fish and the birds made good conversation pieces for some time and then, almost in the middle of a sentence, Lily said, 'Shall we give it a try, then?' I replied that I thought we might get to know one another first and this immediately led to the exposure of the 'companionship and understanding'. 'You didn't think I really meant that, did you?' Once the subject had been raised Lily spoke freely about fees and her need for money. She told me of her girl-friend who had disappeared a year before, taking her savings (£1,628) which she had kept in a small suit-case in a mattress. Lily spoke at length of the necessity of her activities, but stressed it was in no way to be confused with prostitution which she thought disgraceful. She spoke of her clients as friends, although they came from scattered parts and none visited her more than once. Their once-only visits were, unhappily, easy to understand. Lily looked over sixty and could easily have walked out of one of Tennesse Williams's blowsy pieces. Her dress was hanging apart, showing areas of thin skin and sinew. She was continually adjusting her underwear.

Once it was established we were not going to 'give it a try', Lily became even more amiable and garrulous. Like Anna, she had tales to tell. There was the negro who spent two weeks arranging to visit her. He travelled two hundred miles, and appeared with £50. He put it on the table in five pound notes to speak for him. Before he arrived Lily did not know he was a negro. She turned him away 'not because I don't like black men – it's just the colour of their skin'.

One night she had been to a party – a professional engagement – and claimed she was drugged. She came round four miles from home, covered with cuts and bruises, lying in a two feet ditch. In her purse was £25 in addition to her fee for the evening, which itself had been fifty. 'God knows what they did to me – I ached for three weeks afterwards – but I reckon they had their money's worth.'

Because of that experience she was at first reluctant when a client offered a large fee to go to his house. There were letters and phone calls before the actual date was made. Lily was driven to the outskirts of the town. It was a large house, detached and in excellent order. Lily was invited to take coffee in the lounge with the man and his wife. After an hour of pleasant chat the man turned to his wife and said, 'Well; what do you think dear?' to which his wife replied, 'Yes dear, I think I'd like to.' Lily was invited to accompany the wife upstairs. Lily summed it up by saying that the wife had wanted a woman to play with her for more than thirty years. 'We got undressed and into bed. I felt her up a bit – she came off and then cried all over me. It was a bit pathetic really, but, she seemed to enjoy it. She came down quarter of an hour after me and said her husband was to drive me home and give me another £10. I never heard from them again though. Pity – it was easy.'

Lily was a likeable woman, lost in a world she appeared to know little about. Her case, however, raised less pathos than the next.

Joan Hagen

Her advertisement was straightforward and simple: 'young lady would like to meet presentable gentlemen.' At the appointed time I arrived at a house in the middle of a 1930s council estate. The house was in a dreadful state of repair and the small front garden littered with rubbish. The mat by the front door was rotting into the tiles and the path was deep in dirt. As I knocked at the door, there was a movement of curtains and shouting, 'Mam! Mam! 'E's 'ere. 'E's come. It's 'im.' 'Mam' appeared at the door, opened it as little as possible, crept through and whispered, 'Go away. Go away.' I was told to return tomorrow because 'his mother's just turned up and I daren't let you in'. She suggested I should come back that evening, that afternoon or 'in 'alf 'our'.

I said it might be better if we made another appointment and to this Joan readily agreed. My reasons for doing this were simple – I had seen enough to convince me her background was genuine. She had obviously done her best to prepare for my visit, but had no skill in applying make-up, dressing her hair or even keeping up her stockings. My interest in Joan Hagen stemmed from her reply, scribbled on the reverse side of my letter. It was almost illegible.

Dear Sir,

Thank you for your letter, the reason for my advert is I am married with four children to keep, we are in a bit of debt. My husband can not work yet, he is just getting better his muscle system collapsed. We heard of the Book and decided to try to get some help this way. I'm not used to this, and I would only do normal sex, a sheath would have to be used as I'm not on the pill, also I could only spare an hour as I have to see to the children and husband's diets and medicines. I would have to ask at least £5 as we need the money. I am in most times as I don't go out much. I do not have affairs or drink and I do not go out with anyone as I think too much of my husband for that. I am 34 years old 36in–24in–37in. I know £5 is a lot to ask as I am not used to it, but do need money for debts. If you want anything that is not normal sex then I'm afraid I will not be the right person, I am sorry but I am just not used to anything else and would not like anything that is not normal. I hope you understand our reasons for trying this.

Yours sincerely,
JOAN

Her case was more suited to a social welfare document than a contact magazine. It all seemed to be tragically true. Any pangs of remorse I felt were more than atoned for by the case of. . . .

Marie-Chat

'Young French lady will escort you anywhere or will entertain you at home. There is no need to be lonely and discretion is assured.' I replied to the box number and three days later received an envelope without stamp on which I had to pay postage. Enclosed was a printed memo as follows:

> DEAR
> IF YOU WOULD LIKE TO CONTACT ME PLEASE
> TELEPHONE : ...... up till 6 pm. after 6 p.m. ......
> Yours sincerely

I rang the number and Marie treated me to a long description of the weather in London. The telephone conversation was easy in so far as I had only to offer monosyllabic ejaculations to elicit long slabs of supposedly genuine personal history. The lady claimed to be French and her accent supported her claim. She also laid great stress upon her education to university level and her qualifications as a psychologist — suggesting that the latter equipped her particularly well to be an escort for me.

She asked if I was interested in education and amateur theatre. On receiving a non-committal reply, she talked about the necessity for corporal punishment in schools and out of them. It was also suggested I should consider amateur theatricals and the joys of dressing up that stem from them. She elaborated on her collection of martinets, clothes and wigs. She invited me to her flat so that we could talk over the social, psychological and personal implications of our possible friendship. I made an appointment to meet her at her flat in a day or two. I thought that would be the end of the conversation but I was treated to a lecture on the joys of learning French and told I should 'command everything French' since the Common Market would soon be with us. Our conversation had lasted sixteen minutes.

I called upon Marie as arranged. She lived on the seventh floor of a block of council flats. I was tired and looking forward to sitting down (I discovered later there was a lift, very well hidden by a laundromat) but my luck was out. Before I had time to ring the bell or choose one of the three Algerian door knockers, the door opened and I was greeted by an urgent signal : 'Go away'. (I had arrived the moment another 'friend' was about to leave.) To prevent our meeting I was ordered to hide on a half landing. This I did, and, with some impatience and apprehension, waited for twelve minutes.

My apprehension had been ushered in by the sight of the lady I was to come to know as Marie-Chat. A fevered imagination could, with difficulty, conjure the vision of slatternly obesity that came at me from the door of the flat. She was just over five feet tall with long black hair that could not have been dressed or washed for many weeks. Her only garment was an old housecoat with a solitary button. At one time it had been peach coloured but since then had attracted a collection of ugly stains. Marie's face was dark and bloated and what could be seen of her arms and legs was covered in multicolour scratches, cuts and bruises. All in all, Marie-Chat seemed a nightmare figure from the pages of a sensational novel of the French Revolution — no doubt at the time of its worst excesses.

Hiding on the dirty half-landing waiting for my summons was an experience I have no wish to repeat. It took some determination to prevent my leaving without further investigation. (In the event my determination was well rewarded. My session with Marie lasted for more than three hours and provided material more than rich enough to justify my twelve minute watch.)

Eventually I was called and shown into the porch. At first sight it appeared to contain the residue of jumble sale Victoriana, Algerian leather and metal goods. Nor was the porch different from the other rooms. The whole flat was littered. Valuable antiques and worthless trash vied for living space. They had one thing in common – thick dust. Scattered amongst these treasures were hundreds of books. Since there was cheap erotica displayed on a side table – between two dirty tea cups – I expected the books to be similar. They contrasted strangely – half were art appreciation and half philosophy and psychology. (Nietzsche came between a paperback on Pop art and an excessive edition of the history of the Bahaus on one side and Berenson and the Baroque on the other.) I commented on one title. Marie immediately launched into a dissertation on the place of philosophy and aesthetics in an acquisitive society. She spoke lucidly and well. Her flow was interrupted by a thought prompted, she said, by my interest in her as a person. She took me by the hand (actually hand, wrist and arm at once), and rushed me into another room where she delved into an apparently bottomless pile of rubbish. She brought out a badly preserved piece of hardboard on which there was an oil painting of Marie as she might have been some years before. After many false starts, I was told it was a self-portrait.

I was taken, once more by main force, to a corner of the room where there were two cages. Marie released two desert rats and two hamsters. I was invited to handle and caress any or all of them. When I declined Marie held a conversation with them – totally excuding me. She explained my lack of affection by saying I was a man and therefore didn't understand them. When my behaviour had been sufficiently discussed. I was invited to inspect the mouths and necks of the desert rats. Both of them had bite marks and were missing a considerable amount of fur. Marie laughingly told me that, because they were both males, they fought a lot and it was nothing to worry about.

There was a reason for her laughter: in the early hours of one morning she returned from her business in town (at that time still undisclosed) to find the desert rats in a bloody and furry state. She was convinced they were dying of tuberculosis, phoned for a taxi and took them round to a vet whom she proceeded to knock up and inform of the emergency!

The story of the vet put her in mind of medical matters and she parted the skirts of her housecoat to reveal huge legs covered with scars and bruises. Telling me to ignore the obvious ones she pointed to three that otherwise I would not have noticed. They were all that remained of her operation. She was put out that they could be seen at all and explained that if her holiday had been successful she would have been tanned and there would have been no trace, but there had been no sun during her month in Spain.

Mention of the holiday prompted the unlikely follow-up of the photograph album (it might have been a quiet afternoon with tea and toast in Budleigh Salterton). Photographs of the children — a boy aged ten, another twelve and a girl fourteen — were paraded. At last the album came to an end. She put it down with an air of finality. 'There. Shall we have a cup of tea and then begin — or shall we begin straight away?' I replied that a cup of tea would be nice, hoping there would be two more cups somewhere, but the two dirty ones were taken into the kitchen alcove and swilled in cold water.

Tea was served without benefit of saucers and Marie threw herself into an armchair and said, 'Well; what is it going to be?' I replied that I was equally interested in amateur theatre and the French educational system. Marie laughed, 'You didn't believe that surely? Come on tell the truth — I know you are having me on.' I looked at her vacantly knowing she would take any opportunity to talk. She did; and it did not take her long to demolish ideas of theatre or education. 'Amateur theatre' was a euphemism to attract transvestites and 'education system' advertised her talent for corporal punishment — giving and taking; with or without bondage.

This led to more disclosures. Marie told me not to be afraid of anything she might suggest since she knew who wanted what and how much of it and, 'I knew the minute I saw you, you were new and didn't know much.' I asked her how. She claimed a combination of psychology and woman's intuition that never let her down, not even with men who wore toupees. (Marie worried about removing toupees or knocking them out of place because, no matter what kind of dressing or undressing her 'friends' went in for, they were all sensitive about their lack of hair.) She followed this with, 'What's it going to be then?' and suggested a mild bondage. I was about to ask what was meant by mild bondage when the telephone rang. Although Marie ostentatiously went into another room to take the call I could easily hear everything she said:

'Hello, [pause] Hello. Oh! It's you again. I know it's you from your breathing. What are you going to say to me this time? [pause] You'd be excited if you could see what I'm doing now. Yes, this minute. While I'm talking to you. You'd like to see that, wouldn't you? [pause] Oh, well; if you're not going to say anything I'm going. I can tell you're in a bad mood this afternoon. I'm going now. I'm going. Bye bye. Bye bye. [pause] Bye bye.'

Marie came into the room in a great rush and said, 'It's that man again. He must know the children are on holiday because he doesn't ring much when they're at home. He's obviously a family man with a sense of decency.' (In passing she said she didn't mind 'queer' telephone calls since she had studied psychology. 'Everybody's perverted, one way or another. In fact the only abnormality I know is normality.')

She went on to tell me that men treated her as if she ran a confessional. She spoke of Genet, about whom she was well informed, and of fantasy as the basis of reality.

By this time I thought I was prepared for anything. Her story of the dentist proved me wrong. He had paid Marie £25 to sit in his surgery chair, naked. For half an hour she had played with her privates while he watched her through mirrors. Even Marie thought this was unusual – but only for the mirrors, not for the event itself.

It was at this point that Marie decided to initiate me into her rituals and led me by the arm into the adjacent bedroom. Draped behind the bed was an Algerian rug; another, equally beautiful, covered the bed. The ceiling was a mirror. The room was littered with children's books and toys. It was incongruous.

Inside the room I was addressed as 'Sandra' and told that I was a naughty girl for wearing the wrong clothes. 'You are an attractive girl with a beautiful figure and you deserve much more sexy clothes.' (I was dressed in sweater, slacks and sandals.) 'You must feel dreadful in your old dirty clothes. You must change them straight away.' Marie spoke of French underclothes, the sensuous feeling of silk and velvet, and the luxury of lace.

While the chat-up proceeded she undressed me. (After the recent conversation about reality and fantasy, the experience was intriguing, since by common consent we pretended it was not happening.) Marie was not as expert as I would have expected and the undressing took some time. Finally I was ready (naked) to be shown a 'gorgeous collection of expensive underwear brought over specially from Paris'.

The clothes were nondescript and cheap, a pair of directoire knickers and a half slip, both in pale blue lace. I made appreciative noises and Marie dressed me in the two garments. I was then given a once white brassiere, now soiled. It was fitted and I was invited to parade in front of the wardrobe mirror. I made a foolhardy remark about my flat chest and was rewarded by two pairs of smelly socks. Marie stuffed them in the brassiere and told me I was to be strapped to the bed and punished for being a 'naughty wicked girl'. And that I would learn 'not to do it again'. I asked what I had done. 'You know well enough. Don't make it worse – do as you are told.'

I was pinioned to the bed with string, old ties and bits of chiffon. It was not particularly distressing since I could move a little and knew I could undo my bondage. This was little comfort when I saw Marie disappearing through the bedroom door with my clothes. She told me she would not be long and I was to 'behave myself' while she was away. After a short time, Marie reappeared, dressed in a short black leather dress with her face made up in a macabre manner. In her hand she carried a short thonged whip.

I was treated to more accusations of being naughty. This time a specific charge was made. I was a perverted Lesbian; I liked only little girls and I must be punished for it. I was then whipped;

lashed with a leather belt and slapped by Marie's bare hands on
my buttocks. It was painful, and continued for some time. Finally
she stopped and left me with the abrupt instruction that I was
to untie myself.

I did as I was told and had just finished when Marie returned.
Her face was a vision of anger! I was supposed to have known
she was only joking and was now to be punished for trying to
escape. This time I was securely pinioned to the bed — evidenced
by the pain from the tightness of the bonds. It hurt more the
second time. Marie again disappeared — this time threatening to
ring my wife and my office if I did not do as I was told. (It was
an interesting moment of double role playing. She said she had
been through my pockets and had all the information. In fact
there was nothing in my pockets regarding my identity, not even
a phone number.) This time she was away longer. On her return
I was pleased she was in a more pleasant mood. I was offered all
kinds of soothing ointments, words and gestures — the latter
supposed to be erotically stimulating. I was back to being
beautiful Sandra and definitely in favour. It seemed a change for
the better.

I took the opportunity of the change in attitude and atmosphere
to suggest we had a cup of tea. (In retrospect it must have been
a ludicrous scene topped by a ridiculous remark, but it served
its purpose.) Marie said, 'You mean before we have ordinary
sex?' I mumbled encouragingly, being prepared at that stage to
do or say almost anything to regain my clothes and some initiative
in the situation. The ploy worked. I was presented with my clothes
and allowed to dress.

While dressing, I disclaimed any inclination for a further sexual
relationship — ordinary or otherwise — and from that moment the
conversation returned to its earlier style. Marie told me of clients
who were unable to have sex at all, unless they were in a state of
severe bondage. She described it: they were tied to the bed
with leather straps and secured with chains and handcuffs on
wrists and ankles. Their eyes were covered with heavy bandages;
their ears and nostrils securely plugged and in their mouths, held
in place by plaster, a large rubber ball. The ball had a hole for

breathing. Some clients remained in that state for as long as five hours, being whipped at regular intervals. (She mentioned this was lucrative since she could entertain three clients at one time.)

Tea was now ready (the same cups) and I had just been given mine when the telephone rang again. Once more I was able to hear all that Marie said, not that it was necessary since this time she told me the whole of it on her return. The caller was the editor of a new contact magazine who wished to pass on some thirty letters enquiring for someone with Marie's skills. The editor had filled his first edition with false advertisements and was now farming out the replies to real advertisers in other magazines. (I later bought a copy of the magazine. There were over a hundred supposedly genuine advertisements.) Marie told me the procedure was not new and no doubt the editor would also demand a free go. She accepted it all as quite reasonable.

Marie told me stories of titled ladies and international horse-women who came to her to be whipped and beaten. Some of them frustrated by over-considerate husbands and seeking a sado-masochistic Lesbian relationship. She told me of her premises in the West End and the precautions she took with spy holes, double locks and chains, since she did not use a maid. She told me of the occasion when her daughter, at the age of seven, came home early from school to find the outside staircase being washed by a homo-sexual transvestite dressed as a waitress. Marie claimed he was made up well enough to deceive neighbours and the world at large, but not her daughter: 'Mummy—there's a man dressed up as a woman cleaning the stairs—what shall I do?' Marie found it amusing that her daughter had seen through the disguise but also disturbing that she had come so close to home. This, and the following case, were the only occasions when she appeared not to accept her own claim 'only abnormality is normal'.

As I was leaving I remarked to Marie on some of her daughter's dolls that were littered about. This reminded her of life-size dolls. Describing their function in clinical detail she became serious. 'I feel sorry for men who have to use that sort of thing—they must be very lonely.' There was a pause; then 'they must be kinky too!' Experienced as she was, she could not accommodate the idea of an inflatable doll being other than 'perverted and obscene'.

There was no better opportunity for me to leave than with this piece of contrariness. Marie had not previously used the word obscene or perverted. It was a fitting end – for Marie as well as my other cases.

Bed and bawd

Other letters brought something quite different. They came from my replies to advertisements offering weekend accommodation as guests of 'lonely middle-aged couples', who wished to meet 'educated gentlemen for the pleasures of conversation'. They offered hospitality. The following letter is typical.

> Dear Derek,
>
> Thank you for your letter in answer to our advert.
>
> As you will see from the above address I am at present away on business. You may reply to me at the above address. My wife was attracted to your letter and self description and she is quite prepared to accommodate you in my absence. This has my full permission. She is 42 years of age, voluptuous, brunette, quite uninhibited with a dominating sexual urge and has an oral artistry that all who have experienced it describe as the most ecstatic sensation they have ever known. She has a taste for administering mild corporal punishment whilst accompanying it with erotic caresses.
>
> You could be accommodated from a Saturday to Sunday staying overnight on the Saturday. Full meals. All-in cost £20.
>
> Hoping to hear from you,
>
> > Sincerely yours,
> > > HARRY

It was but a short journey now into the world of massage via more ambiguous advertisements.

ANOTHER WAY OF GETTING 'IN TOUCH'?

.The massage business was fascinating. There is no doubt that for some, the massage was a preamble to, or indeed euphemism for, sexual intercourse, but this was not as frequent as I had been led to believe. The usual arrangement is for the client, 95 per cent men and 75 per cent in hotel rooms, to be naked and to receive a full body massage – satisfaction coming from the eroticism of the situation, lived out in fantasy, rather than the actuality of the encounter. In many cases there was no sexual manipulation and some of the masseuses went to great lengths to ensure that private parts were not only left severely alone but were covered by the towels many of them carried for that specific purpose.

Some massages were excellent although expensive. Some were quite dreadful – the masseuses knowing little about the human frame and less about massage. One young negress had cold hands and arrived without oil or powder. Some made pleasant conversation; some went to great lengths to discover if I liked it; some were brisk and efficient and others were just surly.

Half the advertisers were genuine and half made opportunities for a sexual relationship of one kind or another. Of the latter the following show the range of replies.

The advertisement in a well known national weekly, •read 'Massage for gentlemen by appointment.' I rang:

'It's a very personal and private service done by a young lady in her private flat. The fee is £3.50 and if you're interested in anything different you can discuss that with the young lady herself – you know what I mean. It's just those little extra variations, isn't it, love? You can have a personal service for the three fifty – that is if you don't want just the relief massage.* She's got a nice figure with a forty inch firm bust – she'll give you a very good time and won't rush you a bit. . . .'

There was an advertisement that offered exotic delights, oriental

* Relief massage is digital – and sometimes other – massage to ejaculation.

oils and personal attention from Marie Louise. I wrote to the box number and received what I thought was a charming, personal letter from the lady. She asked me to ring.

D.B. Is Marie Louise there?

M. She's busy at the moment but it's Miles speaking.

There are various sorts of massage that Marie Louise does — there are in fact two or three girls here who do do massage but don't read it too far as how far they'll go. There is no intercourse available and no masturbation so. that is quite clear. It may immediately disappoint you I'm afraid, but there you are. The charges range between £3 and £10. With most of the massages all except the £3 one — the girls are covered only in the minimum of bra and briefs. There is a completely private room and you're on a four foot six double bed. While she's massaging you she's on the bed with you. There are in fact mirrors, so you can appreciate her figure. This is what makes it really erotic . . . imagine dim lights, pleasant music in the background . . . very pleasant massage.

It was in fact a large and well run commercial organisation, with HQ and peripatetics — male and female — but specialising in the erotic. By chance it was the next morning I received the following reply giving 'further details' of a private, visiting massage service.

Dear Derek,

Thank you for replying to my ad which is sweet of you. Well the massage I'm offering to give you will be hand massage to every part of the body followed by Electric Vibro massage if desired. I prefer to be topless, when massaging, as I feel so much freer. My fee for massaging is £6 for two hours, of an evening but unfortunately I cannot use my place as I can only visit or meet you, if you stay in London. Do you?

About myself — I'm 32 years, 5ft 1in, brunette, figure 40in–27in–38in. I'm broadminded and very willing to please and be pleased in every way.

There were many masseurs advertising their services to women only. My wife followed up nine, not one of whom was trained or even a professional professional. They all wanted a fee at first, but when pressed, agreed to perform without charge. Some were prepared to travel long distances at their own expense. Their euphemisms were extravagant – a 'personal service that would meet ladies' most stringent requirements' – but inexorably led to offers of intercourse or digital sexual manipulation 'if that will overcome the tension.' All of them claimed their special treatment would overcome loneliness – no doubt their own as much as any client's.

I came across many strange objects and obscure practices while researching the contact magazine industry. All kinds and conditions of agencies and people were prepared to ring, write or send things through the post. The specifics defy the imagination and some of the descriptions make Kraft-Ebbing read like Longford.

If it was sex for cash that was wanted, the market was buoyant and, within its own terms of reference, gave value for money. The goods existed and their price tags were adhered to. Buyers and sellers alike seemed satisfied and the entrepreneurs were making a lot of money.

If it was a genuine personal contact that was wanted, the market was minimal and the goods shoddy. Men in search of a remedy for their insecurity and loneliness would find themselves surrounded by call-girls. Women engaged on a similar search would not readily approach the magazines. If they were to, they might find themselves misunderstood; they might also find they had discovered a remedy. (They would find the same at a nudist resort. The problem is their inability to use the business – a self-defeating mechanism.)

There seems a good case for relaxing the law so that advertisers may state explicitly what it is they seek or offer. As things are, the possibility of lonely men and women being deceived by false offers and misleading advertisements continues.

RSVP
The Personal Column

LADIES AND GENTLEMEN OF THE PRESS

I had always imagined that 'Miss Lonely-hearts', from a different but connected area, was exaggerated. I was wrong. The world of the personal column was a world of sentimental deception – mixing anxiety and amicability in equal measures. It was divided into two polarised groups, almost opposing factions, advertisers and respondents. In a certain way, the twain never meet. In other ways, of course, they do, but even at the primary stage of exchanging letters and courtesies there is a failure rate of about 50 per cent, in spite of the ubiquitous SAE. After this first hurdle, respondents were markedly better than advertisers in sticking to their promises – all my respondents managing to be at the right place at the right time.

There were deceptions from both groups. Two in particular, from advertisers and respondents alike, were not entirely unexpected. They involved women and concerned age and physical attributes. Some attempted to delude with extreme naïveties and naïve extremities : Charlotte, for example, claiming to be forty-eight and proving to be nearly eighty. All the women I met or corresponded with rated physical attributes higher than personality traits – most of them believing relationships would stand or fall on physical attraction exclusively – an irony for those driven (for that is how many saw it) to the last resort of the personal column.

I started my research with a local paper. One issue carried seven advertisements from 'ladies and gentlemen'. This particular paper placed an embargo on the words 'men' and 'women' and would print no age under sixty. The advertisement manager explained that ages and numbers could signal improper intentions. He claimed to be extra-sensitive at detecting such signals, and others like them. He was a victim of self-deception. I discovered personally that he failed to prevent the interchange of 'improper information'. The first discovery took me unawares – I had been slow to get the message. (Later I became more expert, perhaps too expert, since I began to wonder if there were ambiguities or *double entendres* in Situations Vacant : 'Wanted – garage attendant : must be good with his hands.') The advertisement simply read 'Lonely, youngish lady needs friends.' There was a box number. It led me to the case of. . . .

Miss Peele

I wrote her a letter which I hoped was *juste milieu* – certainly more neutral than enthusiastic. Within twenty-four hours, Miss Peele rang and I was invited to vsit her at home. (I was later to find such invitations at least significant, if not overt, signals. In the face-to-face business there is every chance that a normal courtesy will be taken as a 'come-on'.)

Her voice on the telephone combined cultivated vowels with a slight tremor that might have warned of advancing years. So might the difficulty in hearing me which she attributed to a bad line. The tremor also added to a general impression of hesitancy and apprehension. Once again I should have got the message. Later, I quickly recognised the tell-tale inflections of unattractive women making assignations under the false pretence of being physically attractive – pointless deceptions, since capable of exposure even before contact is made. (But many lonely people lead lives of continuing deception. True, they are not unique in this. In general, few of us will confess to bankruptcy – in money, morals or relationships – but with the lonely, deception of self and others is often forced upon them by their self-defeating condition. They will refuse to admit their loneliness or their fear of it. Sad, because, for many, admission would help relieve the condition.) At the time, I merely thought Miss Peele sensitive and cautious. We made an appointment for three thirty on the afternoon of the same day.

She lived in the basement of a decaying Georgian house. I went through squeaking doors into an entrance lobby and found the board that displayed a list of tenants. Miss Peele's name was absent. I inspected the foyer for a note and rechecked the tenants' board. I was still looking at it when I was approached by a woman of about seventy – highly made-up and wearing a tight woollen trouser suit. She asked if she could help me. Her voice was soft and charming. I said I was looking for a Miss Peele. 'I'm Miss Peele. Will you come this way?' She led me through a maze of passages, kitchens and bedrooms to an untidy bed-sitting room where we formally introduced ourselves and I was presented to Miss Peele's cat. The introductions over, I wondered what I was going to say to this unlikely 'lady' who was dressed and made up in the style of someone fifty years her junior. As it happened, there was no problem. Miss Peele needed only minimal responses to her nervous chatter.

She talked of the weather and her opinions of the feet and legs of passers-by. (The only window in the basement room gave onto the footpath.) From time to time she fiddled with the radio – an antique model with knobs, lights and a clock – changing programmes in search of pop music. Her alternative pastime (she never once stayed still) was to move her cat as soon as it settled. During the displacement activities of small talk, radio and cat fiddling came naïve questions about three subjects: her figure, her charms, our immediate future. No reply was needed, Miss Peele never paused, and only looked at me when she thought I couldn't see her.

'Are you disappointed? Well – what do you think? Do I need to slim? Am I older than you thought? Do tell me – I shan't be offended. What kind of girl are you looking for? You'll have to tell me what you like – because I'm very shy. You don't mind shy girls, do you? I often go for a little lie down in the afternoons, do you like that? Is that naughty of me? Do you like naughty girls or nice girls?'

After half an hour I was invited to take tea. 'China – with a little lemon. It's the only kind I can take. Its good for my figure.' More incongruities: Miss Peele put on a beautiful lace apron and brought in a valuable silver tea service. On an equally attractive tea tray were cracked cups and saucers and an opened bottle of milk. I was offered a chocolate biscuit from a scruffy paper packet. Mine had slight touches of mildew.

Towards the end of the tea interval Miss Peele told me I had been the only person to reply to her advertisement. Shortly afterwards she told me that was not quite right – there had been one other, but she 'wished it had never happened'. It appeared a 'boorish man' had sent her a long letter describing the delights of nudist colonies. According to Miss Peele he did so in 'unrepeatable detail'. He had also been inspired to send a 'vivid sketch' of what Miss Peele would look like unclothed.

Miss Peele cleared the tea tray. When she returned she asked me if I would like to dance. I murmured that dancing was not my forte. Miss Peele was not put off so lightly. In spite of me disclaiming interest she 'helped' me to my feet and began to gyrate around me. I stood quite still but this did not deter Miss Peele. After minutes of complete immobility I clicked my fingers unenthusiastically in time to the music. Miss Peele responded: 'There you are – you're marvellous. I said you would be, didn't I, and you trying to have me on.'

I continued with the finger clicking. Miss Peele found another response: 'I can tell from the look on your face you're excited. You are, aren't you?'

Before I had time to reply she executed a couple of pelvic thrusts; stopped dramatically and for the first time, looked at me face-to-face. 'We can do it if you want to, you know. Do you?'

I grunted non-committally; I wanted to be certain Miss Peele meant intercourse. I did not want to jump to an impossible conclusion and hurt her feelings or make myself appear more foolish than I already felt. She saved me by spelling it out and asking for 'a little present'. I asked her what kind of present.

'Money, of course! What else should I want?'

She would not name a figure; always referred to it as 'a little present'; but insisted it must be money. There was no uncomfortable hiatus. Miss Peele had a lucid language flow and made three points:

(i) There were plenty of permissive, promiscuous girls about – therefore I should give her a present.

(ii) There would be no love in it – therefore I ought to give her a present.

(iii) Too many men got away with too much anyway and 'a girl has to learn to be hard' – therefore I must give her a present.

Then things took an unexpected turn – Miss Peele broke into tears, repeating 'It's not fair – it's not fair.' She was a terrible yet pathetic figure, combining the tears of a spoilt child and the sentiments of an emotional pubescent in her seventy-year-old frame.

The tears stopped abruptly and Miss Peele said: 'I suppose this is the end then?'

After this plastic dart Miss Peele settled into a calmer state. I was shown courteously – if with an attempt at over-exquisite manners that came out fey and sour by turns – to a large, hanging curtain I had thought covered either a window or failing plaster. Miss Peele swished away the curtain. I was at the front door. The labyrinthine route we had first taken had been a ploy to ensure Miss Peele could inspect me before making contact – or disclosing her room. I left by the front door – depressed by the reality but pleased to be quitting the façade.

Marjorie

The advertisement read: 'YOUNG LADY (late twenties) wishes to meet gentlemen (30–45) for friendship.' There was a box number. I replied in a neutral manner and within twenty-four hours received a telephone call from the advertiser, during which she described herself as of medium build, not unattractive and with short mousy hair. She said her age was 28.

We met. She was fat and 4ft 2in. Her hair was medium brown and shoulder length. There were two topics of conversation: her children and her exhusband. I attempted to raise alternatives — they were all turned inexorably to the original two.

It transpired that her children were 17 and 13 and over a period of time it became clear that she was 38 and not 28. I listened for nearly three hours to stories of the childrens' accomplishments, interrupted only by lengthy descriptions of her ex-husband's deficiencies. There were even some tears for her failure to cope with them. She had a talent for self-expression in a form that required no more of a partner than he should have ears.

I had hardly spoken during the evening and we never achieved a moment's real contact but Marjorie was adamant that the evening had been an 'unmitigated success' — her words!

Betty

The advertisement read: 'Am not attractive, permissive, self-centred or rich, but 42. Is there an unattached tall male, 44–48, with car who would like to meet me for outings and companionship?' There was a box number. I replied in a neutral manner and within twenty-four hours I was contacted by telephone and a visit arranged.

There was much talk on the telephone as to where we should meet and how we should recognize one another. Eventually a neutral venue was agreed and I was told to watch out for a slim lady with red hair and blue eyes, five feet two inches tall. A cloak of anonymity covered any further identification, and I was informed I could call the lady Betty.

I arrived as arranged to find Betty in the company of another lady — both eagle-eyed. The second lady (Betty's sister) tried to hide behind the corner of a wall to watch the proceedings. The incident was not unfunny.

The advertisement was genuine and exact. Betty thought it safer to advertise than to reply since 'you can tell all about a person from their handwriting'. She was apprehensive about physical contact and did her best to keep at least six feet from me during the evening — in an hotel lounge. Her husband had left her seven years earlier and now her son was about to join the army. 'This seemed the only way of making companions. Other people are lucky – so why not me?'

Bertha

The advertisement read: 'Young lady needs gentlemen friends.' There was a box number. I replied in the usual neutral manner, giving name, address and telephone number.

It was three weeks before anything happened. Then there was a succession of telephone calls, but it was not until the seventh that I was in. The caller gave her name as Bertha and immediately began to apologise for not being in touch before. She had had second thoughts about answering her replies but had become so depressed she had changed her mind again. She hoped I didn't mind.

Bertha volunteered her reason for advertising.

'I did it because I have these bad feet. I've had bad feet for two years and it was beginning to depress me. First it was athlete's foot; then it was corns; then it was an infection of the ankle. After that it was a parade of things, all of which were cured without my feet being any better. Then they sent me to Guy's to have my stomach operated on – they said there was a blockage – but my feet were just the same. It got so I couldn't walk or stand and I had to change my job. I became so depressed that all my friends left me and I didn't know what to do – I was just sitting at home every night getting on my sister's nerves. In the end she moved out, so I was all alone, and still worrying about my feet. It was then I thought 'Why don't I advertise?', so I did and then I had second thoughts because of my feet. Am I boring you?'

The end came in a rush and tumble. I was asked, and agreed, to write to her as soon as I could. She blurted out her name and address in a fit of apparent embarrassment – at the same time pleading with me that I should not call upon her at the address she had given since 'I am alone at nights and not able to defend myself properly because of my bad feet.'

There were many others I met through the medium of the personal column :

The woman who invited me straight into her home and spent four hours telling me how her husband and daughter had died within the previous six months. Her son had married and gone to Australia. Her cat died soon afterwards and 'the dog spent every day looking at his master's chair. That was his chair. Look, there are his slippers – the dog's lying on them.' She had advertised because she felt unable to make men friends at work or in a pub. 'Anyway, I just couldn't go into a pub myself, and if I went with another woman, that would make it worse. You see two women look like . . . I don't know what – it's just misunderstood.' She thought that by advertising she might 'explain my position to a sympathetic man without him thinking me neurotic or a whore'.

Throughout the evening she tried to talk about other things, but was obsessed by her bereavements. She was a charming and attractive woman. I hope time has relaxed and released her.

I met seven self-confessed teachers – 'self-confessed' since they thought teaching would put off attractive men and bring offers only from (their words) 'self-seeking, lazy, good-for-nothings'. Not one of the seven wished to meet a male teacher and they all felt marriage to one would surely end in disaster.

There were women who concealed the fact that they had children. One advertiser had five. It was not until we had spent five hours together she said: 'There is something I think you ought to know.'

There were many who claimed to be divorced and turned out only to be separated. I met three who claimed to be separated and who were in fact living with their husbands.

There were those looking for extra men friends and a good time. They used the personal column for two reasons: it was a way of meeting new people without fuss; it contained an element of excitement. One girl, who looked no more than seventeen, said 'you never know who you're going to meet and it's much more fun than the telly. It turns me on no end.'

I ADVERTISE

When it came to respondents there was a great variety. I advertised twice in a neutral manner : 'Lonely but not unattractive gentleman would like to meet pleasing lady for companionship.' To these advertisements I received not a single reply.

I made the wording less ordinary. 'Writer, attractive and in early forties would like to meet friendly girl.' This brought in over thirty letters in a few days. (Replies came in as long as three weeks after publication.) A few were from cranks. (Some were from social groups for the lonely or separated!) The majority were from lonely women looking for a male friend. Only two replies came from women who had not previously answered advertisements (one woman wrote to at least three each week). I spoke with many on the telephone, wrote to some and met a few. The following cases give a fair cross section. . . .

Charlotte

> Dear Advertiser,
>
> My husband died nearly two years ago, since when I have all but become a recluse. I assure you at times it is almost unbearable, for I am exceedingly attractive and may I say interesting?
>
> My home is lovely and I have a dear little dog, but it is not sufficient for a woman of my ilk, I long for some pleasing companionship, also to go out and about, for I have some lovely clothes which just hang in the wardrobe for as you know it's impossible for a woman to go *anywhere* alone.
>
> If you are interested please ring me any morning after ten, (I get up late now) or any time you choose, except lunchtime, when I go shopping with my little dog.
>
> I wish to remain anonymous, for who knows? You may live near me, you might even be a neighbour! So I'm sure you will understand.

Should you ring just ask for Charlotte, which is my second name – I of course will answer.

Sincerely,

CHARLOTTE

PS I sincerely hope your appearance is pleasing.

I rang.

C. Hello.

D.B. Hello. This is D.B. Is this Charlotte?

C. Yes, it is.

D.B. You know who I am?

C. Yes, I do . . . it's very awkward isn't it? One doesn't know how to start. I know your name now. I didn't really mean to write 'Dear Advertiser'. I don't know what came over me. Frankly, I was very embarrassed. Well . . . now what happens?

D.B. Perhaps I might describe myself? ·

C. Good.

D.B. [I give a brief description]

C. Good. Yes . . . I didn't expect an Apollo or Adonis or anything like that, but you know what I mean. I just want someone who is pleasing to look upon. Now I am a little older than you . . . but don't be frightened, it's the fashion today for ladies, I'm glad to say, to be a little older than gentlemen.

D.B. How old are you?

C. Oh! I'm forty-eight. But there is one person, now don't laugh will you, please? He's precisely twenty-eight – I'm old enough to be his mother now aren't I? Well, we met last Christmas – and he begged me to go about with him. He's an interior decorator in Hampstead – I said, 'you must be joking'. He said, 'No, I'm not joking.' I said, 'Good Lord, I'm old enough to be your mother.' He said, 'I think you're fabulous.' But I thought I'd tell you that, because it is the fashion. But really I'm very very young in my ways and I wouldn't be a day younger in this day and age. I've got some lines but I've got lovely features, beautiful features.

You know, a lovely face really. Although I say it myself. Well I've prepared you for a few little lines but a lovely face . . . and a beautiful figure – sorry to say that again, but I know that too – you see. My beauty isn't quite so striking as it was when I was younger naturally, but it is beautifully shaped you understand. Beautifully moulded my face – I know that because – well I can't tell you why. Right, now I suggest we should meet and size each other up. Now, I like the sound of your voice.

D.B. Thank you.

c. Mine is very low – usually if I answer the phone to any stranger they always say 'Sir', which is very convenient, I often pretend to be a man you see – with this low voice. . . .

We arranged to meet in the car park of a public house near where she lived. Charlotte said, although she was not afraid of me, she would not have me in her house until I had 'passed muster'.

While it was hardly possible for her to live up to her own description, she was an attractive woman, but her careful make-up and beautiful clothes could not make her look younger than sixty. (From the ages of her friends, relatives and children, as well as from her being married in 1912 (in Venezuela) I gathered she must be at least seventy-five. I gave her full marks for preservation, but none for the attempted gambado.)

Eventually she invited me to her bungalow. It was a pleasing home – filled with valuable antiques from all over the world. Charlotte had a poodle that she treated one moment like a small child and the next like a lover. She told me of her life and loves and spoke most of the time in soliloquy and continued quite happily *without reference to me*. There was never a dull moment – even if a quarter of the time was taken up by Charlotte's self-adulation. Her vanity was boundless, and her language unusual. She spoke of men 'worshipping at this shrine' and 'not letting any man desecrate this shrine'.

In complete contrast was :

Mona

> Dear ???,
> Your ad, was fascinating. I think we have a certain magnetism. I felt it from the column. Ring me.
>
> MONA

I rang her. We never met, but talked many times on the phone. We touched on Yoga, Zen-Astrology, Hamlet, and even did a crossword puzzle. One of the clues prompted Mona into describing herself as a 'disorientated, unbalanced, misplaced Oriental, whose vital statistics were an empty head'.

She told me of Age and Time and Life and Re-incarnation and Spiritual Restoration and Physical Resurrection and (neatly closing the circle) invited me to a spiritual encounter group. Unfortunately there were only two meetings left and I couldn't make either.

In contrast again :

Connie

The letter was straight to the point :

> Dear Writer,
> In answer to your advertisement.
> I am not your scene but you sound like mine. My name is Connie. I am 28 years, have long dark hair and passable figure; also I am of a friendly disposition, who is longing for a companion of a completely different nature to that of which I am accustomed to, there is however one drawback which I hope won't put you off. I am married, but my husband works away a lot, so I have plenty of free time. The only time it is unwise for me to have phone calls or dates is at the weekends, otherwise I am available, so if I could possible be the one to fit what you are looking PLEASE phone.
> Hopefully,
>
> CONNIE
> PS I love life and want to enjoy it without any strings.

I rang Connie and we arranged to meet. She took me straight to her home where we spent the evening chatting pleasantly and fussing an ageing Alsatian and a three-month-old kitten. There were interruptions: the telephone rang nine times. The ninth call was from her husband. (It was important he should be spoken to, his whereabouts checked and his next move discovered!) It was a mildly disturbing position. Eight phone calls had been enough – Connie swore they were from girl friends, but it seemed unlikely – the ninth was an *embarras de richesse*.

The evening established, as her letter had suggested, that Connie was looking for sexual adventure. She made it quite clear she would be interested in groups or parties I might take her to. There was no deception – to me. Connie wanted an affair without strings but her husband must not know. She was adamant that her marriage should 'remain secure and stable'.

I have placed this report last because it is symptomatic of the world of the column: honesty and frankness in one area, expert deceit in another; the need to confide and the wish to hide; the wish to be trusted and the fear of believing; the fear of failure and the urge to relate. Above all the urge to relate. RSVP? SOS? 'Not waving – drowning!'

END GAMES

While there is much that is parasitic, fantastic and fabulous in the face-to-face industry, there is more that is undeniably factual. Behind the façades and myths lies a real world with real people: people who use a real organism to provide a real service.

It is easy to claim the service is not in the public good; easy to criticise the owners for profiteering and accuse them of wickedly manipulating the lost, the lonely and the innocent. It is easy – too easy. It is also hysterical and unjustified – a gratuitous and ungenerous attack on the industry and a pre-judgment of its customers.

Of the hundreds I met, only a few felt they were being swindled. The rest were convinced they needed the service; that it was doing them good; and that the prices were reasonable. I disagree on all three counts, but this may be condemned as special pleading, since my excursions into the intimate personal confrontation industry were not motivated by a sense of inadequacy or fear of loneliness but by the wish to write this book. (Encounter wizards will no doubt draw their own perceptive conclusions about my 'massive rationalisation'.) I used the services as a disinterested observer – albeit from the inside. Since the services are tailored to meet the expressed wishes of those who are interested, converted and in need, it is not entirely to be unexpected that my conclusions differ. I am convinced that if I actually had had the need I would have been swindled. But this is a snake-eating-tail process and a matter of personal conviction.

A matter of fact is what I paid while surveying the scene, and it was the going price for everything I sampled. In real terms I believe I got value for money – personally and professionally;

but if my needs had been what they were supposed to be I would have felt cheated. This IF, however, is crucial to the market's existence and central to the organisers' justifications. It seems appropriate — I for irony; F for fantasy.

Some organisers claimed that if the clientele were different then so would be the service. They were undoubtedly sincere, since they were either dedicated to an idealistic position or sensitive to the main commercial chance. As things are, the services are built to the requirements of customers who share some marked personality deficiencies. Accepting that I was a common factor and there may be some distortion of selection arising from that, there was still a remarkable degree of coincidence in the specific traits displayed. The clients all showed signs of a listless, fatalistic futility in their self images and were more than lacking in flexibility and drive. This did not manifest itself in a marked sense of inadequacy or absence of confidence but in a passive state of waiting for the gifts of personal relationships and bonds of affection to descend. A rigorous view might suggest there is a strong dose of laziness in all this and that they expect the world to come to them, without any conscious effort or inconvenience on their part, once the service (magazine, agency or personal column) has been set in motion.

It is ironic that, having decided to use the service, their self-awareness does not take them to the next step of using properly what the service supplies. They expect the service to do all the work while they wait for a fully developed end-product to emerge — without effort or apparent concern and still unaware that it is this failure to take an active part in interpersonal relationships that very probably brought them to the business in the first place. Most of them seemed completely ignorant of the status-building-and-reduction exercises that organise and express one human being's thoughts and feelings for another. The look in the eye; the interested raised eyebrow; the body images of receptivity; the nod, smile or monosyllable that registers approval or at least understanding — all these tools of building up the image of a partner were absent. In fairness, it must be said they were also absent in reducing the image, but in the early stages of a relationship the lack of a response can be more deadly than a lively display of hostility. Most of them seem consumed by a condition of humble arrogance: a passive 'Take me or leave me' attitude that did not fit at all comfortably on one who had approached an agency asking for help in making contact. It seemed tragic and ironic that, having diagnosed the need for help and confessed it (implicitly if no more), they were unable to read the symptoms properly and begin to attack the cause of their malaise.

One agency paid lip service to the need by adding a footnote to its letter of introduction: 'Remember: Be Interesting – Be Interested.' Unfortunately, the agency took their suggestion no further. True, the thought of Clinics for Deficient Personalities leads quickly to satire and nausea, but the need is real.

One group of people partaking of the services available were quite different from the rest. They were to be found among the encounter enthusiasts and were the opposite of the passive 'ready to receive' types. They were hostility merchants – carpetbagging their aggression from group to group, searching for opportunities to parade their active arrogance in a way they were not able to achieve in their day-to-day lives – or so I optimistically hoped, since any regularity in that behaviour would have been most unpleasant for the recipients. Fortunately for everyone concerned, these characters were happy to live in the fantasy of the specially structured groups of encounter devotees and did not turn to the magazines or agencies. Intimate personal confrontations with them would no doubt have been painful.

But apart from the aggressive encounter types, the people I met in search of contacts were more-or-less normal: they had jobs (many of them well paid and responsible positions); they had relatives and children with whom they seemed able to relate without traumas (some I met in domestic situations and found the times to be pleasant and without dramatic or offensive incident); they shopped and dealt with the business and administrative sides of contemporary life without apparent strain and they were aware of most of the events that the media consider important. They were not obviously psychotic and had no more than their fair share of headaches, ulcers, indigestion and constipation, but many were worried about being frigid or impotent. I formed the opinion that these anxieties were no more than symbolic of a general state of frigidity or impotence and it was easier for them to focus upon and confess to the specific sexual anxiety (by no means uncommon) as a self-contained cause than to see it as a specific symptom of an overall condition. Once more the interest in symptoms excluded attention being paid to causes, and further showed the irony inherent in the whole area – a concentration upon superficialities : creating the problem initially and preventing its later treatment.

Most of the people using the contact agencies or an equivalent knew exactly what they were likely to get, and preferred it to direct personal action. Such a course of action may be self-defeating and immature, but it destroys the condemnatory suggestion that there are many lost, lonely and innocent people who are victims· of ·ruthless, commercial manipulation. The industry mounts no large-scale campaign of advertising. Commercial radio and television carry no flood of seductive, bargain-offer panaceas. There is ·no door-to-door distribution of leaflets, nor is there an organised sell of any kind – hard or soft. Most of the advertising matter is carried by journals devoted to sympathetic material, or in the ubiquitous personal column. The advertising copy is discreetly worded and quietly displayed. Most customers actively search out the agencies and are well aware of the quantity and quality of service likely to be offered.

It is only a minority who are deceived, but it is a substantial one made up of first-timers, anxious hopefuls and fretting optimists. Most of them, in all probability, will be inexpert in semantic conceits. This lack of specialised expertise is a major pitfall, for in the contact business discretion and ambiguity jostle for position. Idealistic proprietors have no wish to insult or hurt the feelings of potential customers and commercial fringe operators wish to steer clear of police investigations. Both phrase their advertisements with delicacy, hoping to combine promises of undreamed of bliss with guarantees of sincerity, security and discretion. This can be a deadly combination, for, unless the customer knows exactly what he wants and where to look for it, he may be offered, instead of a continuing, concrete personal relationship, a series of interrupted, ambiguous, abstract liaisons. Under the customer's very nose the discreet will have become discrete.

The novice is in a difficult position and there are many traps surrounding him. This is unfortunate, since there are individuals who, through no fault of their own, find themselves temporarily in need of a helping hand – the kind of hand many of the agencies claim to hold out. Because of the vague terminology and the many inexactitudes of intention displayed by some agents and clients alike, the chances of the newcomer finding the appropriate, temporary niche are few and far between. It is much more likely that he will find himself on a band-wagon of futility – *in contact* with those who will not or cannot be bothered to make the effort of direct personal action and *in touch* with no one.

Nevertheless, the services of the contact agents are demanded by customers who prefer them to be exactly as they are, are happy to pay the prices asked and who will adamantly maintain that the services are needed – in the words of more than a few 'desperately and sincerely needed'. There are certainly enough clients to keep the agencies profitably busy, and turnover seems to be accelerating. The reasons for this, as put to me by customers, are twofold: the relaxation of some social and sexual conventions makes the activity less of an object for contempt, satire or remark and the growth of urban alienation makes it more of a necessity for survival. Whether from idealistic or commercial motives, the contact services seem likely to be with us in growing numbers for some time to come.

Having accepted the demand, if not the need, for person-to-person contact through factitious organisms, it is unreasonable and irrational to complain of the concomitants. In particular it is irrational, after offering to pay for some of the benefits of social intercourse to be offended by a personal offer of a specific kind. Having accepted the principle of making personal contacts, building bonds or establishing companionships by paying for the initial moves; having accepted the principle of placing the self on public display or advertising for bids, it is not mature to object to the logical adjuncts – unpleasant and distasteful though they may be, on their own account, to some.

Since irrationality and immaturity are part of the human condition, the industry will continue – and no doubt flourish – praised by some and criticised by others. Deception and hypocrisy will continue to make it difficult to achieve an objective assessment of the services and the people who use them, for there are few customers – be they sophisticated swingers or sad lonely-hearts – who will let on to an outsider that they make use of such services or agencies. Certainly there are even fewer who will state openly that they use them. Yet agents and clients alike will, in confidence, deny any such anxieties about possible stigmas – even claiming that they have all but disappeared – and cover with a rosy glow of virtue (on the strength of a doubtful necessity) any sense of inadequacy, shame or guilt regarding their connection with the person-to-person business.

And business it is, ranging from one-man cottage industries to large national networks. One operator runs an agency from his front room in a terrace house. He claims he does it 'because I feel sorry for lonely people'. He is a steel-worker, lives by himself and occupies all his free time in 'helping people find one another'. He charges 25p per introduction and his income from this can hardly cover his expenses. It is not difficult to see his agency as no more than a displacement activity for his own lonely state.

The literature he puts out is stencilled and duplicated in his own front room and carries the stamp of inexpert operation – different from the expensive glossy publications from the larger houses with many well paid staff. Some of the brochures are large and impressive and make much of their computerised techniques. (The staff of one such agency told me, however, they felt like bank clerks must feel about the money they handle, 'Well, it's not quite real, is it? I mean, you can't get to grips with them as people, can you? Well, not from a form anyway – and not when we deal with so many.' So much for that particular agency's claims of a sympathetic and personal service.)

Most of the well presented literature comes from houses that are soundly established – registered companies with permanent addresses. There are others with constantly changing names and addresses and others that lead any enquirer a will-o'-the-wisp trail from accommodation address to accommodation address. (A secondary income is made by many managements from running an accommodation address service – for their own clientele and for the chance customer in need of such a facility for his own purposes. Not all the cases I checked ran their books in the way common sense suggests and many innocents, wanting to make a surprise of an informal visit, must have been left to feel something of Theseus' experiences with the maze and the Minotaur.)

The less reliable managements are easily recognised from the cheapness of the paper on which their publicity is printed, the faults in reproduction techniques and the frequent bad spelling and grammar. These are the businesses that run one contact magazine and describe it differently dependant upon where they are advertising. The innocent reader is given the impression the contents are directed exclusively at (say) naturists or music lovers or homosexuals. In fact, not even the title of the magazine or the covers are changed. There are those with different covers and titles but with identical contents. (During one month I bought four 'different' magazines – all at 50p – to discover the contents were the same.)

As might be expected, these managements were also difficult to trace and almost impossible to contact. Of the three I managed to interview, all were 'in it for the money – what fucking else?' None of them was pleased to have been traced or prepared to be interviewed. The more permanent managements were more polite when approached personally, that is, when I approached them in my client role. Some went to great lengths to enter sympathetically into my situation. It may even have been sincere. It was at least patent that they were making an effort to give my case 'personal consideration'. They went out of their way to be accessible and friendly. One manageress even gave me her private ex-directory telephone number, 'Just in case you feel you need a friend at any time. Treat me like a sexual Samaritan, if you like.'

Other agents covered the operation with sticky charm but were not skilled or patient enough to be able to disguise its pseudo element. They made the occasion feel like a visit to the dentist. Others treated me to an abrupt refusal to communicate in any way other than through the post. With one or two, my requests for personal guidance were met with rude dismissals. Refusals to communicate thoughts or feelings were a regular rejoinder to my request for help or information when I approached agents as an investigator. There was always plenty of charm and a super-abundance of brochures and copies of letters from satisfied clients, but no direct contact and no sign of empathy.

One factor almost all agencies had in common – from the most sleazy to the most idealistic : whatever the type of agency and whatever its line, 'ladies' – especially if under twenty-five – would be treated with care and offered privileges. Most of the time this meant a reduction in fees. Sometimes this was half price and very often the service was entirely free. Women's Lib enthusiasts may find the situation objectionable, but the market is undeniably all in the woman's favour. The treacly tones in which some agents addressed themselves to women between eighteen and twenty-one made me wonder if there was still a strong market for virgins. Youth and nubility were at a premium and the overtones combined the puritanism of the Victorians with the salaciousness of White Slave Traders.

Many magazines are issued free to women; men have to pay the full price – at least for the first copy. This price varies enormously. Some small magazines – twenty-four pages 4in × 3in – cost £1, while much larger publications are on sale for as little as 8p. The average price is just over 50p if bought at a book stall or sex shop. But later, once on the circuit, the special offers and the subscription lists bring the prices down to nearer 10p. The purchase of a magazine however, is only the beginning of the expense. .

The reader will find he has to pay not only to advertise but also to reply. Advertisements are charged at the average rate of 4p per word. Many agencies insist on a minimum payment of £2, except for women who are frequently allowed to advertise free. (Women get another bonus. Many magazines offer a special facility to their readers – for an extra charge men may precede their advertisement with the words REPLY FREE. This service costs about £1 and is supposed to *guarantee* many genuine replies. I placed the REPLY FREE slogan in front of four advertisements asking for female companionship and received no reply. This may prove nothing about the REPLY FREE principle, because the four were part of twelve advertisements I submitted. They all appeared monthly for at least three issues and brought no reply.)

Replying to advertisements can also be an expensive pastime. In addition to the obligatory SAE, the agencies charge an average fee of 25p per letter, although they offer reductions for bulk replies, some of them quoting charges for bundles up to fifty.

If the replies my wife received are any indication to the state of the general market – and my conversations with other 'ladies' who use the columns suggest they were not above average – there are many operators who are making a lot of money for very little effort. For example: over a period of a month, as a result of one advertisement in one magazine, my wife received no fewer than eighty replies. Since the magazine in question was hand-duplicated on cheap paper and the replies came in bundles through the second-class mail there were few expenses (and probably fewer overheads) to be deducted from the income of £20. Later, in reply to a 'Couples' advertisement, we were to receive – over a period of three months, more than three hundred replies – an income of £75.

The magazines in which these advertisements appeared carried over two hundred entries and, while it is impossible to know how many were genuine, it seemed likely that almost all would elicit replies – if they contained a reference to the availability of a woman, with or without an 'attached' male. Since the magazines can cost, at the outside, no more than 5p and the turnover of some is extensive, I can see no reason to quibble with the editor of one who claimed he was making between £800 and £1,000 each week. Little wonder the contact magazines are an expensive way of making contact. By comparison the contact organisations offer a more economic service and are less likely to lead to persons of either sex – but especially females – with a financial or even professional interest.

With the contact organisations there is much variety in the scale of fees. I have been offered ten 'absolutely guaranteed' dates for as little as £1 and one only for as much as £25. The equation of averages, including enrolment fees and reductions for more than one date, was: one date achieved in the flesh = £1.

Some agencies offered lists of clients wanting to make contacts. The lists themselves appeared to be inexpensive – over two hundred *guaranteed* names and addresses for 20p. It was only when I came to invest time and more money (postage, including the SAE) that I found the cost, in real terms, of failing to discover a contact was extremely high. I counted myself fortunate that I had not, in addition, invested high hopes and emotional intensity – since the return (just nothing through the post) would have been more than hurtful.

I interviewed some of the people who advertised for friends through the agencies' operating lists. Experiences seemed constant: the chances of receiving a reply to a letter written to an advertiser are very slim. The major reason for this being that once the advertiser actually gets responses through the post the exercise has achieved its purpose and the continuing trickle of letters confirms the attitude – there is something to look forward to each week (and with some, it is every morning) without further effort, further personal exposure and the risk of rebuff at a real confrontation. The possibility of contact is there and the advertiser no longer feels totally alienated – after all, she could have had all those friends, *if she had really wanted*. The opportunities have been made and there is no longer any fault to be found with the advertiser. In real terms it seems very much a self-defeating mechanism but in comparative terms, from the inside, it represents achievement and fulfilment.

The duplicated lists and their initial inexpensive rates produced a one hundred per cent failure rate and it was not long before I knew exactly what to expect from the agencies that operated that way.

There were also the lists and brochures of 'attractive events'. The initial enrolment fee was not high – between 50p and £1 –

but the results were just as disappointing as those from the friendship lists – nothing! The pattern of personality characteristics seemed to be similar to those in my non-event meetings with personal contacts – complete preparedness to sit back and let others make the effort, in this case arranging events, but then not to take advantage. Symptoms replace causes and appearances replace realities. It is not the event that is wanted but the availability. Opportunity seems to be the flattering unction needed for the souls of subscribers; the events themselves are shunned, and the shunning is disguised through complicated rationalisations to do with (most frequently) colds and headaches and 'other things cropping up'. Local organisers have similar tales to tell all over the country. Their lists contain many subscribers who continue to retain their annual membership but, in spite of reminders and telephone calls, never appear at an event.

The situation is different in the cities – London, Toronto, New York – where there are more people with genuine needs and desires to make contacts quickly and for a limited time. Events in the three capitals are better organised and better supported, although they too have their passive subscribers, some of whom the organisers have never seen or spoken to.

Many other lists and brochures came through the post. Some I had requested and others were a complete surprise. I received lists of models and escorts, pen-friends and 'unique personalities with different interests – just like yours!'. Unless I had requested *and paid for* the lists they would omit some crucial piece of information so that it was impossible to trace the individuals described. Many of them were worded in the ambiguous phraseology that I had come to recognise as typical cover for the professionals, so I did not pursue them.

Three special offers I did pursue. They seemed so unlikely to be genuine that they justified investigation. Each offered me a list of names and telephone numbers of males and females who were anxious to make new friends. The lists were each to contain no less than one hundred *absolutely guaranteed* telephone numbers for £1. (Two of the offers came from London and one from New York.) Payment was required in cash. One list arrived two months after I sent the money. I am still waiting for the other two. (I tried to trace all three from the original address but gave up after discovering that each went through at least two accommodation addresses.) Close inspection of the one list showed that many of the telephone numbers were duplicated. One number featured twelve times with a supposedly different girl. I rang the numbers and found that some must have been picked at random from the phone book – or even made up – since the subscribers were unaware of the list or their presence on it. (I followed one enquiry through and the subscriber was happy to pursue it to the level of police and GPO. I presumed this was sufficient evidence to guarantee his genuineness.) The active numbers turned out to belong to professional males and females.

One agency, defining itself as 'very exclusive', offered me five telephone numbers for £10. Over the telephone the principal made it clear the ladies would offer and require the 'little extra'. The advertising material had described 'ladies and gentlemen of superior education' looking for 'friends, companions and respectful and respected escorts to help overcome that temporary loss of connection'.

The average subscription to the agencies offering lists of people wanting to meet people was in the region of £2. They covered pen-friends, platonic companions, escorts for mutual help as well as overt sexual relationships. In theory it is an inexpensive and discreet way of making contact. In practice it brought no result that I could not have achieved more quickly and cheaply by consulting one of the many display boards offering me dancing lessons, French, or lady's riding kit for sale.

The rates of friendship and marriage bureaux also varied considerably. Some offered their full and complete services, *until satisfaction or marriage*(?), at a once only fee of £2. Others had an enrolment fee, a membership fee, or a separate fee for each introduction. Some had all three. Many had special rates for special circumstances: age, sex, part of the country, marital status. There were sections for those 'separated but not divorced'. (Needless to say the additional fee for this section was high – between £10 and £20.) Some offered to arrange the dates; some only to give names and addresses; some offered private consultations – and for an additional fee were prepared to visit my home to make a better diagnosis of my needs. Some agencies quoted HP terms.

The membership fees varied from £1 to £25. The average was about £10, but this counts for little since the variations in service were considerable. One agency made an additional charge in the case of marriage – £20 – and, if the marriage were not reported to them fourteen days before it took place, an additional £10. (Since the initial fees were nearly £20 their claim to charge 'lower than the average bureau' was interesting.)

The charges for parties also varied considerably. There were closed parties with free admission, 'just bring a bottle'. The fee, however, had already been paid by affiliation to an organisation which charged the maximum for a listing – £10. There were socials with admission charges varying from 25p to £10. One agency had a good line. For introducing a newcomer the following 'free credits' were offered for parties : a male – one credit; a couple – two credits; a single female – five credits. The alcohol always flowed freely and the usual charge was £5.

At meetings of more esoteric groups – meditation, contemplation, religious – there was always a big welcome with little charge. At most it cost 50p and much of the time, as a newcomer, I was introduced free of charge and there was little pressure to practise or even accept the philosophies of the movements.

A dramatic difference of ethos and finances emerged from the encounter groups run on a commercial basis. I was placed under real pressure to conform to the ideals of the movement and to continue and develop its practices from my first meeting. For groups setting themselves with ideals of self-determination and, above all, 'You do your thing and I'll do mine', it was fraudulent. Sophisticated, subtle and seductive in its techniques but fraudulent in intent – particularly for people who placed such apparent importance on honesty of responses and self-awareness.

No such pressure was evident or implicit in the non-commercial (and, in the main, non-professional) encounter groups. Here, there seemed a genuine, if woolly and misguided, attempt to help people to relate, with many leaders using their own homes, offering hospitality and making no charge for attendance at meetings. At other meetings the only charge was for refreshments. When an admission fee was asked, it was no more than reasonable – between 15p and 50p.

The commercial encounter groups operated on an entirely different budget. The charges varied: £6 for a twelve-hour session in London, $250 for five days in Montreal and New York and one 'on-going' group charged an hourly rate of £2·50 – 'students' could attend and leave when they wished, merely clocking in and out and paying the appropriate fee. Many groups required a non-refundable deposit of up to 50 per cent.

Some of these commercial, professional groups were also run in semi-private houses and accepted up to twenty-five members on any one course, employing only one leader. It seems unlikely that overheads, salaries and expenses could eat away all that much of one day's income—not when it reached the notable total of £150.

All in all, the face-to-face business is expensive: in time and money and energy distinguishing genuine from bogus; in time and money and energy on the telephone (I checked on my telephone calls and charges and found the average time taken to arrange a meeting with a non-professional contact was over thirty minutes); in time and money and energy in correspondence (not forgetting the SAE). Above all, the high failure rate from bogus advertisements eats away time and money. There are those who do not bother to reply as well as those whose advertisement is a cover-up for a commercial deal. Even with those who do reply, there are many advertisers who place more than one advertisement in a magazine or entry in a brochure or registration with an agency. (The agencies do their best to prevent this but pseudonyms and accommodation addresses are easy to arrange.) Many advertisers not only duplicate their advertisements in one publication but also in different magazines.

Whatever time and money is wasted by these ·pitfalls is in addition to that already invested in form filling and initial subscriptions. Some of the forms take considerable thought and effort if they are to be completed properly. The results did not suggest they were studied by the organisers to serious purpose. They frequently led to incompatibility. Sometimes this was discovered on the telephone and sometimes by letter. Sometimes it was not until a meeting had taken place that the realities emerged.

Even telephone calls and letters could take up a lot of time: not enjoying the freshness of a new relationship but in unravelling the smoke screens with which many advertisers surrounded themselves and their lives. Time after time I had to listen with enormous concentration to discern the subtleties of language flow that would signal a differential between what was said and what was meant. Time and again I had to re-read long missives to determine whether the form and content signified anything more than a wish to write long letters.

Much of my time was spent talking on the phone or reading and writing letters while many *apparent opportunities* to meet were being overlooked or lost through some trivial reason. After a time it became quite clear that many advertisers were using the agencies in order to have people contact them, by phone or post, but without any intention of arranging a meeting. It seemed ironic that these advertisers should use the contact agencies and not the correspondence clubs, since they would have seemed to have suited them better. After further time, and some experience of the failure of the pen clubs to deliver the goods, I realised there was sense in their manœuvres even if they were annoyingly deceptive.

It may be argued that advertising, telephoning and letter-writing about making personal contacts are sufficient and necessary to the ritualistic destruction of loneliness. They can only succeed, however, when the individual wants the promise of contact but not the existential reality. Rituals are for ritualists. People who need people – as opposed to those who want to know people are around, within hailing, smoke or other signalling distance – are not to be satisfied with the vicarious pleasures of substitute, displacement activities. The rewards are too few, the mechanics too complex and the finances too high.

IN RETROSPECT

The least expensive and most efficient organ of the person-to-person business is the personal column of a local newspaper. For as little as 4p per word it is possible to make many contacts — most of whom will be genuine and some of whom will bring unexpected delights and pleasures. (Ironically, replying to such advertisements is by no means so sure of success. But its failure rate is no higher than that of the other methods and the cost is considerably less.) It was through the personal columns I met the most appealing and attractive personalities of my survey. I did so quickly and inexpensively. (If this were a consumers' guide, the personal column would certainly achieve a five star 'Best Buy'.)

The friendship groups and the clubs for the lonely were generally anything but their titular claims and were, in the main, dull anathemas — time and money consuming non-events, organised by non-leaders for non-people.

I spent my happiest times in the doing, making, thinking, being groups. Here I received a large return for little investment — provided I was happy to plough my resources back into the groups and not hope to carry social energy and relationships into the outside world. As a groupie, in the group, I was well served. It was when it came to bridging the gap between the esoteric and the exoteric that the system failed to help. Groupies wish to remain groupies. They claim 'That is what it's all about' and they have something of a moral to point. They had, however, much more to offer, at less cost in time, effort and money than the commercially organised parties which were like group events for lost gregarians; mere socials for ciphers. The parties were at least harmless and had nothing in common with the organised sessions of hanging-out hysterical hostility — redolent of some of Orwell's visions — engineered by some of the professional encounter group leaders. I left most of those meetings with a serious new-leaf-intention to get on better with my neighbour's mangy cat — a small gesture of personal control to combat the Big Things of 'Encounter Me, Man!' (The end-product was in fact worthwhile, so the groups may not be entirely without merit.) If I left the encounter groups with some despair it was of a smaller proportion than the disappointment brought by the contact organisations. High hopes repeatedly dashed were my lot in this area. The major consolation, if any, was that most clients do not enrol with high hopes and seem to have smoothly functioning efficient mechanisms to prevent disappointment. (It may be cynical but the ninth beatitude has much to recommend it: 'Blessed is the man who expects nothing, for he shall never be disappointed'.) Generally, the agencies require too much time and money to be invested for the little real return they offer. But those clients who use them, consciously or not, as substitute and displacement activities are more than satisfied with the results they achieve.

My hopes were not high when I enrolled with the correspondence clubs and it is just as well for my disappointment would have been greater than with the contact organisations, and with them I actually made a number of initial contacts, if no more. In spite of all my letters (not forgetting the SAE's) I received not a single response.

I did not delve into the marriage bureaux in a way that invited client response, and from my external assessment of the spirit and techniques of the agencies, I am glad I had no cause to. The feelings that stay with me are total bewilderment that a satisfactory match is ever made and a deep conviction that clients must approach agents from a state of despair, otherwise the publicity brochures would immediately kill further interest in the business. The riddle-me-ree language of fragile, rosy delicacies must surround any transaction with a web of ambiguities sufficient to create complete lack of trust between arranged partners – no matter how long their liaison may last.

Any web of ambiguities woven in the marriage markets becomes plain by comparison with the mirror-images of deception and intrigue to be found in the world of the contact magazines. There was an extremely high investment rate for the nil return achieved by my personae in their quest for what appeared to be advertised. They were constantly led up the paths of non-existent gardens.

For myself, as writer and playwright, the return for time, money, emotional and nervous energy was excellent. For any subscriber who knows what he wants, knows how to describe and recognise it and knows the moves to make in order to realise it, the returns will also be excellent. The rest must beware fantasy, intrigue, deception and tangled webs and prepare to spend time and money with no guarantee that they will be able even to handle the goods.

The organisations and their networks cover the country. The clientele is increasing. The manipulators' rewards can be rich – avariciously so. But while many of us remain desensitised by a sense of inadequacy or anaesthetised by fear, the industry will flourish – its services used and its captains well paid.

To criticise the symptoms and leave the cause untouched is part of the human malaise. Many of the industry's most savage critics are themselves lacking in sincerity, generosity and compassion – all major targets for their attacks. One of the reasons for this is also a reason why the industry is alive and well and living all over the place : society has developed microcosms that are too small, tense and possessive (nuclear family units) within macrocosms that defy individual understanding (national units). One remedy is for the latter to become smaller – an unlikely possibility – or for the former to grow. Communes seem a step towards creating a society – not a family and not a nation – in which individuals can be, grow and relate without the neurotic tensions that can spring from the family or the inhuman, nihilistic, isolation that can stem from the state. Other steps would cost high in endeavour but low in cash. The rewards would be high in relationships and low in cash – BUT (particularly relevant in our acquisitive society) :

'The rich get rich and the poor get poorer.'

Alternatively, 'To him that hath shall it be given and from him that hath not shall it be taken away'.

These two thoughts sum up the essence of the person-to-person business.

Although there is increasing social and sexual mobility in Western society, the people who are benefiting are those who are already mobile. They can more easily wander further and faster. Those who found it difficult to take the first step still find it so. The freedom to cross frontiers is of no value to people immobilised by anxiety or inadequacy and, apart from the manipulators and the professionals, most customers I met felt anxious or inadequate. The fault may be theirs, the state's or the system's. If to Toynbee's definition of town life — 'Anonymity, Alienation and Anomie' — Anxiety and Anger are added, then town life certainly becomes a major target. None of the cases I met lived in the country.

The young adult seems to get most out of the new machinery for social and sexual mobility — many having found a sense of personal freedom and a satisfying service. For the not-so-young-adult the machinery fails to provide the mobility and flexibility for which many are still searching. For more than a few, nothing has changed; it is merely new acquaintances in old habits. The machinery exists, but there are many who are afraid to approach it or who know how to use it properly — and it was for them, initially and theoretically, that it was created. Only those already personally flexible, and therefore without particular need of the industry, appear able to make full and effective use of it. The irony is similar to that of non-attenders and non-writers belonging to friendship groups and pen clubs.

With the no longer young I found little evidence of mobility or growth and came to despair of the lonely ever meeting in a mutually constructive style or situation. Time and again I heard : 'I don't want to sit at home by myself', 'I like company', 'I like people', 'It's better if you know somebody, isn't it ?'

The question of 'knowing somebody' came up repeatedly. Those who mentioned it most seemed unaware that a prerequisite was a working knowledge of the self. Most of them had little self-knowledge and less self-awareness, and no thought that a touch of either would have improved their situation dramatically.

This message — 'Not until we know ourselves can we hope to know one another' — was superficially important to encounter enthusiasts. (It *should* have been to the contact agencies unless their forms were mock objective tests or plain pseudo.) The message is valid but its place is the breviary and not the public placard. It is better suited to a still small voice than the amplified echoes of encounter and contact.

Inflation is, however, a global problem: inflation of many kinds. The encounter movement claims to burst our balloons of fantasy, let out the hot air of pseudo status and help us examine the residual reality. In fact it merely creates new balloons – the 'frank, ruthless, exposure' balloons – and these it inflates with the emotional hot air that is plentiful at group meetings; these it slashes to ribbons 'before our very eyes' and it is the torn and somewhat grubby latex skin that is paraded as the 'Essential, Real, Inner You'.

(At group meetings there are those who will lull you into a comfortable companionship and approach you with love in their eye-to-eye. They will proceed to unlatch your shoes so gracefully that, unless hypersensitive, you will not know what they have done. They will effortlessly, and quietly, take the shoe from your foot and creep away without word, whisper or whimper. Removed from your presence they will beat themselves about the head with your shoe and burst into tears of *real pain*. On their return, bloody and weeping, they will tell you, gravely and sincerely 'You kicked me.')

Labyrinthine routes of deception and self-deception are virtually the only paths through the jungle of the person-to-person business. From encounter groups, contemplation groups and talk it over groups come the phrases: 'What is your fantasy?', 'Tell me your fantasy', 'Let our fantasies relate'. For an activity based on face-to-face relationships it is ironic that faces are hard to find. Mask to mask, make-up to make-up – these encounters are numerous. But the mask behind the face or the face behind the make-up are seldom shown and rarely seen. The fantasy is almost total. Self-deception is practised by manipulators and manipulated alike. For agencies promoting 'real relationships' and for people searching for 'true friendships' it is a sad picture.

A major tenet of many discussion and encounter groups is that people must be 'broken' before they can relate in honesty. (The Duke episode – 'Let me break him' – is a dramatic example)[1]

[1] See page 58.

Breaking someone else down to build up the self brings only comparative increase in stature. In real terms it may mean reduction. I prefer to believe honesty to be constructive, compassion to be supportive, and breaking needed for neither. I have never thought of human beings as eggs nor their relationships as omelettes – rather the islands they are often said to be (or not to be) in the enveloping ocean of life. We can get in touch in all kinds of ways: rockets, life-lines, power boats, submarines, even swimming. What we cannot do is walk on water. Failing to recognise islands or ocean is often fatal, but it is what many self-help groups intently do.

It is sad that many groups purporting to help overcome personal problems should in fact exacerbate them – the precise achievement of many clubs and groups for the lonely. Groups gathering under such banners succeed less well in overcoming isolation than do those whose objects are, initially or apparently, quite different. The potters and photographers, the contemplators and mystics, the do-your-own-thing-art-and-craft-vegetarians offer better opportunities of making viable relationships – their objective correlatives beng efficient and sufficient catalysts. The groupie organisations expressly aiming to improve the human condition often depress or exaggerate it. The 'Lonely?', 'Divorced?' type gather their members and bore or deflate them. The 'Encounter me!', 'Relate to me!' type, gather theirs, and with equally laudable intentions but more sophisticated methods, take them to hothouses where the organisms of their personalities are cultivated out of proper proportion. The choice seems between spiritual morgues, emotional incubators and the oldest profession. In her excellent survey of the encounter movement in the States, Jane Howard has the following to say:

'The answer, I think, is not to express feeling so much as to recognise it. Group philosophy – wise group philosophy, anyway – does not prescribe that you run to inform your old landlord that everyone secretly thinks he's effeminate, or your boss that you've always thought he was a stupid tyrant. The aim is first to know, in your head and below it, what you think and feel, and then to reflect on newly unearthed alternatives to your accustomed ways of being. Once it is unlocked, the door between your feelings and the cosmos need not be kept yawning open. It can be left ajar.'[2]

Her remarks obtain equally to the alienated lonely; the committed confrontationist; the do-your-own-thing-with-us enthusiast and the swinger — sophisticate or tyro.

Failure on the group side of the business is of a different kind from that on the contact side. Many of the agencies just do not deliver the goods. This in itself is not too serious since personal study and market research can expose those of doubtful origin. What is more difficult to expose or counteract is the self-deception (leading to partner deception) stemming from vanity and fear.

Deception of another kind is a root cause of the high failure rate on the magazine side. It is motivated less by vanity and fear than by society's crippling hypocrisy in all things erotic. The deception can only be exposed by learning the language of the velvet underground — a language so difficult that it is impossible to use the publications without danger of misunderstanding or being misunderstood.

The lowest failure rate is to be found in the personal column of the local press — provided you adhere to the contradictory rules which make it safe, proper and worthwhile to advertise while hardly so to reply.

But it is in the other areas that the money is being made. The nationwide contacts of manipulators and entrepreneurs provide a lucrative network of easy cross-reference. There are, no doubt, some agencies operating exclusively within their own clientele, but most are in close touch with the rest, and it is an easy but sure financial touch.

During my research I spent over £400 in initiating person-to-person confrontations. I can count *on the fingers of one hand* those people who were what they said they were within the bounds of reasonable descriptive ability. Perhaps others are

[2] Jane Howard, *Please Touch*, New York, Dell Publishing Co., 1971.

luckier – though my researchers show otherwise – and perhaps it is possible to make meaningful contact through the machinery without emotional, physical and financial exhaustion.

At the end of my journey there are three incidents that constantly nag me. The first came from the City branch of a well-known bank. I had replied to an advertiser in a contact magazine. Its very high fees were, they claimed, a guarantee of 'absolute confidence and discretion' through their 'fail-safe channels of communication'. My letter came back accompanied by a brief note from the Bank manager. It expressed his apologies for having opened my letter *which had been delivered in error.*

The second concerns a middle-aged man whom I came to know as 'Kalahari Fred'. He was so touchingly pleased to speak to my wife and me twice a week from a public call box that I cannot forget him saying 'It's just nice to hear the sound of your voices.'

The third began with a plain sealed envelope. It was addressed to one of my personae known only to an agency that guaranteed (yet again) absolute confidence. Inside was the following advertisement:

LIFE SIZE INFLATABLE DOLL!

Just Add Air – Life-like in EVERY DETAIL. FEATURES :. Flesh-like vinyl body; Inflatable; Wears size 9 clothes; Clothes interchangeable; Floats in water; Stands 5ft 4in tall; Measurements 36C, 24, 36.

for playful adults

Judy, the inflatable doll, is made of strong, durable vinyl that feels soft and smooth like the lovely girl from whose body she was fashioned.

INFLATABLE : just add air and she's ready for real action.

'My soft, life-like body is flexible and bendable. Let me be your loving companion. I'll live with you when you're at home – sit beside you as we travel in your car – even be your swimming buddy (I float). I know you will love playing with me. Send for me today and my many talents and personal attractions will be all yours to enjoy.'

A covering letter told me I could introduce her to my friends and have 'no need to be lonely or frustrated again'. Judy cost £12·50.

In the fullness of time she arrived – in a brown paper parcel, opened and resealed by the Post Office. I inflated her as instructed. Judy was a disturbing sight : arms without hands; legs without feet; and her face printed on rubber with ears where her neck should have been. As for being 'Life-like in EVERY DETAIL.' – however interpreted – it was impossible, even with the total suspension of disbelief, to discover anything similar to a female frame, and difficult to imagine precisely for what she was a surrogate.

I dressed Judy. (My wife refused to have anything to do with her.) An inflatable doll is difficult to handle. Judy became a major undertaking since the advertiser's claims for her figure were entirely untrue. I took her out in the car, into hotels, restaurants, shops, cinemas, buses and trains. I introduced her to friends as well as strangers. The result was always the same – white faced shock and nausea which lasted for at least three or four minutes and often more than thirty. Some people were interested in the detail of her fabrication. Others just left – some politely and all speedily. She was acceptable to none. What is more, I was rejected by many who immediately concluded I was unsound and unsafe. Even those who stayed to be told of my research were sceptical of my sanity. They were justified. Judy is so misshapen and bizarre that no one could reasonably desire her – in any way.

As a companion, Judy was a failure. She offered no facility for private pleasure and introducing her to anyone was likely to cost their acquaintanceship. Her price was high. I had to buy a wig, since she was totally hairless and had none of the features for which I might have bought her. She has lived in my study ever since – a symbol of our permissive, acquisitive welfare state's understanding and compassion.

The most recent incident has done something to alleviate the sickness she usually conjures within me. The milkman on his normal weekly call for cash said to my wife : 'Cor ! ! I reckoned your old man had done you in. But I looked through the window and thought "Thank Christ ! It's not 'er !" '

Judy and the letter delivered in error could easily have led to blackmail or ridicule. I could have been an eminently suitable case for the treatment – an easy victim of guilt, fear and shame. These three feelings are central to the condition of many customers of the person-to-person business, making them easy victims of the manipulators' skills – usually practised from behind secure cover. Those manipulated can be frail, easily duped and feel inadequate. They can resort to the agents only after their unaided efforts have resulted in failures which have exhausted and depressed them. The causes of the failures remain unchecked. The business provides a treatment which, by its very nature, feeds the snake-eating-tail spiral of symptoms, and social attitudes do not permit an older person to approach it without noting that apparently normal people manage without it.

Hope for the future seems to lie, as usual, with the young adults. Many appear able to use the business houses of contact without anxious feelings of inadequacy and this suggests the underlying malaise itself may soon come under attack. It is a disease that destroys individuality – eroding personal dignity, pride and joy. There are two types of germ : the neurotic possessiveness and pettiness exemplary of many nuclear families; and the hypocritical puritanism and authoritarianism typical of schools. A permanent remedy is simple :

'Astride of a grave and a difficult birth. Down in the hole, lingeringly, the grave-digger puts on the forceps. We have time to grow old. The air is full of our cries. But habit is a great deadener.'[3]

All we have to do is listen – and hear.

My intention has been to report on the person-to-person business from the *viewpoint of the subjective consumer*. It is there-

[3] Samuel Beckett, *Waiting for Godot* (Faber 1956).

fore not a comprehensive objective survey, since I approached it consistently as an *interested participant*. It is personal and direct.

The onlooker may see most of any game, including person-to-person, but the player does the dribbling, tackling, kicking and scoring. He gets the here-and-now winning and losing. He gets the exhaustion and sense of loss when the encounter is over. He is forward, half-back and goalkeeper in one; he is shinpads and boots and his person is the ball. He is the referee of a game played on an unmarked, shifting pitch. The rules change from game to game as well as during the game itself. Every match is played away and there is no such thing as a 'friendly' – everyone knows it's a needle affair, a Cup Final. Only for a few is it ever a loving cup final affair. The rest must be content with draw after draw – and no bitterness because there is no trainer, and they have to pay for admission. The gate is a world of strangers.

'We die to each other daily.
What we know of other people
Is only our memory of the moments
During which we knew them. And they have changed since then.
To pretend that they and we are the same
Is a useful and convenient social convention
Which must sometimes be broken. We must also remember
That at every meeting we are meeting a stranger.'[4]

[4] T. S. Eliot, *The Cocktail Party* (Faber 1963).